BLUE SKY LIVING

THE ARCHITECTURE OF HELLIWELL + SMITH

LIVING

BLUE SKY LIVING

THE ARCHITECTURE OF HELLIWELL + SMITH

Edited with
an introduction by
TREVOR BODDY

Foreword by
TED CULLINAN

images
Publishing

Published in Australia in 2013 by
The Images Publishing Group Pty Ltd
ABN 89 059 734 431
6 Bastow Place, Mulgrave, Victoria 3170, Australia
Tel: +61 3 9561 5544 Fax: +61 3 9561 4860
books@imagespublishing.com
www.imagespublishing.com

Copyright © The Images Publishing Group Pty Ltd 2013
The Images Publishing Group Reference Number: 1005

National Library of Australia Cataloguing-in-Publication entry:

Author:	Boddy, Trevor.
Title:	Blue sky living : the architecture of Helliwell + Smith / Bo Helliwell; Kim Smith.
ISBN:	9781864704815 (hbk).
Subjects:	Architects—British Columbia.
	Architecture, Domestic—British Columbia—Designs and plans.
	Architecture, Modern—20th century—Designs and plans.
	Architecture, Modern—21st century—Designs and plans.
Other Authors/Contributors:	Cullinan, Ted; Helliwell, Bo; Smith, Kim
Dewey Number:	728.0222711

Edited for Images Publishing by Driss Fatih

Designed by The Graphic Image Studio Pty Ltd, Mulgrave, Australia
www.tgis.com.au

Pre-publishing services by Mission Productions Limited, Hong Kong

Printed by Everbest Printing Co. Ltd., in Hong Kong/China
on 140gsm GoldEast Matt Art paper

CONTENTS

6   Foreword by Ted Cullinan

8   Introduction: The Life Well Lived by Trevor Boddy

24   Blue Sky Thinking by Kim Smith and Bo Helliwell

26   Blue Sky Living: The Projects

NARRATIVE

28   Booklovers' House

36   Comet House

44   Ucluelet Aquarium

PLACE

54   Harbour House

60   Hill House

66   Ridge House

STRUCTURE

74   Miracle Beach House

86   Fishbones House

92   Dunlop Point House

TECTONIC

94   Oak Grove House

104   Rainforest House

110   Bridge House

114   Bench Spiral House

SYSTEMS

116   Solar Crest House

122   Gullwing House

124   Deer Path House

COMMUNITY

128   Assiniboine River House

134   Chesterman Beach Homes

138   Wakefield Beach Homes

142   Biographies

146   Blue Sky Architecture 1990–2012

147   Selected Bibliography

148   Acknowledgements

148   Photographic Credits

FOREWORD

by Ted Cullinan

I am writing from a different planet: a planet in which our latest job is to gently squeeze some more houses and flats in to a 1950s and '60s housing estate while removing some of it and civilising it, urbanely. There may be similar situations to be found in Vancouver but that would be very much to do with it as a typical city, which of course it is not; for Vancouver at its northern and western edges or suburbs borders on one of the largest rainforests on earth, containing some of the tallest trees on earth – a truly phenomenal landscape of seasides and inlets, mountains and valleys, high meadows and cliffs and glaciers too; and covering a lot of it is this truly amazing rainforest, in which there are places within a few miles of Vancouver's suburbs where no human has ever set foot.

It is this territory where most of Bo Helliwell and Kim Smith's architecture is built and it is this territory that in part inspires it. In their mature work, round dressed log posts visibly support beams and joists which in turn support undulating roofs which are like rhomboid green canopies, as if the ground is raised to a new level, a truly lovely device, invented by them.

Their work begins on Hornby Island in the early 1970s. Hornby Island is an established farming and fishing community with plenty of good topsoil and fields. It was a favourite of hippies, self-sufficienters and build-it-your-selfers in the spirit of those times. It was from this milieu that Bo and Kim emerged; and they emerged to do some private houses on the island. The Dunlop Point House was designed by Bo and his previous business partner, Michael McNamara, and although its straight-through plan is influenced by the great Arthur Erickson (for whom they had both worked) it contains in itself much wonderful detailed round-wood post construction, which is prophetic of their later work.

Other houses of this period experiment with various forms, as is so common with young architects, from the rather forced symmetry of Gullwing House to the really joyful collage of the three-storey Bench Spiral House. By the 1990s, it is as if the curled-up masculinity of this House had unwound itself to make Fishbones House, an extremely elegant level ridge, off which round roof beams rise and fall down to fenestrated curved walls, to create varied spaces below: kitchen, living spaces, bedrooms, garage, porch and so on. This house is one of the sweetest combinations of expressive visible construction and interpenetrating space making that I know of, anywhere. The Miracle Beach House takes this system and gives it a plan, which is a segment of a circle; Booklovers' House completed the oval implied by the segment of the house into a complete protective courtyard to create a sense of place on the wild island upon which it stands. Harbour House backs onto a cliff and its excellent three-storey SW glass and timber elevation overlooks a harbor with great but controlled constructed grace.

There are many other houses that I could describe, including their Bridge House, which are built below single curved roof canopies, but I want to finish with a description of their public building, the Ucluelet Aquarium. The previous buildings I have described are on forest, mountain or seaside sites and respond to their situations for themselves. The Ucluelet Aquarium sits beside (or hovers over) the harbour and the harbourside buildings of a small community, and it does so most elegantly. A curved-sided triangle sits on its own legs at the town end of the harbour and two primary beams form a minor triangle within the larger one. Joists span from upstands on the primary beams to curve-topped walls on either side, creating a lovely gentle wave-like planked roof. All is made from local timber used in the Blue Sky style of posts and beams waving. It sits quite beautifully at the end of the harbour, gently contrasting and thereby enhancing the ordinary buildings behind and beside it. Its blue is a beautiful, calming shade of blue.

I would love Bo and Kim to design more public buildings, maybe even in downtown Vancouver, for this building shows a great talent for dealing with existing built places.

The final pages of this book show two seaside developments: the Chesterman and Wakefield Beach Homes. The Wakefield scheme includes a very elegant site section, which promises all houses a sea view and proper natural ventilation, with floating curves of metal and flat green roofs. I look forward to seeing it soon and I'd love them to practise and advance this type of work.

Bo and Kim have produced powerful and elegant work all their working lives: it is high up in the world – what Kenneth Frampton calls Critical Regionalism. Long may it last, for we will all benefit if it does.

London

Ted Cullinan CBE, RA, RIBA, HonFRIAS, HonFRAIC

Ted Cullinan studied at Cambridge University, the Architectural Association and the University of California, Berkeley. He established his office as a co-operative in 1965 and received the RIBA Royal Gold Medal for 2008. He was awarded the CBE in 1987 for Services to Architecture, elected a Fellow of the Royal Academy in 1989 and an Honorary Fellow of the Royal Incorporation of Architects in Scotland in 1995. In 2005 he was awarded a Special Commendation by the Prince Philip Designers Prize for his outstanding lifetime achievement in design and in 2010 he was made a Royal Designer for Industry by the RSA. In 2012, Ted was appointed an Honorary Fellow of the RAIC. With the help of friends, he has built six houses, including his own residence in Camden Mews and the beloved Gib Tor. His buildings, writings and exhibitions have generated global coverage and influence.

THE LIFE WELL LIVED

INTRODUCTION

by Trevor Boddy

There is a singular, sinuous line of fine houses shaped by Kim Smith and Bo Helliwell through some of North America's most dramatic landscapes. Like a woodwind solo drifting through a mountain valley, these houses play a continuous melody marked by theme and variation in cedar, stone and timber beam. The continuities of texture, layout and outlook between these houses are quickly evident, but more interesting are their differences, the dappled reflections, the unexpected echoes and the layers of architectural sound drifting through the trees.

Blue Sky Architecture has a "house style" in every possible sense of that phrase, but as I have got to know their work over fifteen years, I now look forward to "house difference" – those inflections, deformations and eruptions of innovation that add a dash of difference to what at first seems the same. The differences between their houses – noting the linked repertoire of surface and detail within their domestic design opus – are revealing, but I found myself asking, after getting to know them better, "revealing of what?" The answer that has emerged, the singular notion that links these residences of varying size, budget and locational character is that they are all dedicated to one thing: the notion of "The life well lived".

As philosophers have struggled with the concept since the era of the ancient Greeks, the notion of "The life well lived" is far from simple or the same for everyone, everywhere. The key to the life well lived is not money, as with the possible exception of a few unusually determined ascetics, being without money is not the key either. Education enriches experience, but perpetual education is a prison of another kind, as legions of over-extended perpetual graduate students can attest. Nature is a garden of delight, except for those times when it is a vortex of terror, and families are the source of warm renewal, except for when they are an un-relieved distraction.

Bo Helliwell and Kim Smith have an uncanny ability to get at the sense of what clients are really looking for in their lives, then deliver portions of it as architecture. Empathy is a word that is almost never used in the critical literature of architecture, but it should be, because empathy is an essential quality for any domestic architect who would wish for their creations to attain lasting significance in the estimation of clients. Seeing through the eyes of clients, understanding their interests and activities, listening behind their words, walking in their pattern-worn shoes – these are all ways of transforming what could be merely publishable houses into livable homes. Architecture schools are places of IQ over EQ, but it is that quotient of emotional sensitivity that is key to the houses collected in this book. Because of a long-term friendship with Bo and Kim, I have been able to track the design of many of these houses from hearing about their first encounter with potential clients, to accounts of initial site surveys (a crucial step), hearing about dialogues over dinner that reveal the real needs of a design commission, to eventual construction and occupation. That Blue Sky's houses are well built, conserving of materials and energy and respectful of their largely sylvan settings are givens, and delivers on the number of bedrooms needed, the integration of gardens and views and wishes for radiant stone floors or double-sided fireplaces, among many other design features.

As we worked together to determine which houses would be included in this volume and which left out, and then grouped them by such thematic rubrics as "narrative" or "tectonic", I started to have doubts that our approach was missing the real story here. That story is one told by their clients themselves, many of whom I had met on my first or second visits to the houses we eventually selected. Nearly all were happy to describe how their lives had been enriched by Blue Sky's architecture, often in unexpected ways that had seldom come up in chats over the sketch designs or cardboard models of the design phase. The body language of these clients told the story, and their appreciation was there for all to see. My doubt about this book was the realisation that we three may have wasted our time spending months compiling and editing the descriptions here of their houses – structure, construction, interior finishes, layouts and relationship to site, by relying only on our account of these projects. As no other architects I have written about, the whole story of Blue Sky Architecture could, instead, have been told in the words of their clients, not their two designers with me along as an outside set of architectural eyes and editor. While a "Blue Sky in the words of their clients" may have been desirable, it was not practical, mainly because a need for privacy is one of the most powerful keys to the lives well lived of these clients. When I interview owners of houses designed by most (but not all) "starchitects", they speak of their new dwellings grandly but with distance, as if they were bits of furniture or a car collection. Not so with the Blue Sky owners, and I respect their clients' need for privacy because they, after all, have chosen to live in these largely rural and sometimes isolated locations.

THREE HOUSES WELL LIVED-IN

If a monograph in the voices of homeowners can't be done, in its place I instead offer a tour of the three houses that Helliwell and Smith currently own and live in – seasonally, sequentially, complicatedly. The three houses say a lot about this pair and their lives before and after becoming partners in life and architecture. The three residences exemplify their ambitions, tastes and most of all, their own, personal sense of the life well lived. The two rural houses – one in the mountains, the other at the beach – are portfolio pieces – treasured icons of the

lives of Bo Helliwell and Kim Smith before they began collaborating. Their current urban house and architectural practice studio is a hybrid between city and forest and a true synthesis of both designers' sensibilities. It is a Mid-Century Modern house and garden designed by others, but enhanced by an utterly different but complementary new studio wing fashioned in Blue Sky's distinctive idiom.

Above: View to downtown Vancouver from the West Vancouver studio/residence of Helliwell and Smith

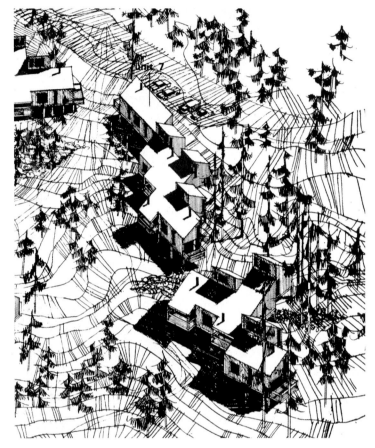

Just up a hill on the main road from Hornby Island's ferry dock, Kim Smith bought her waterfront home in 1985 for its west-facing vistas towards Lambert Channel's low-tide beaches and the snow-capped peaks of central Vancouver Island. Perched on a steep path down to the beach, and with renovations added by Smith, this modest 1970s recreation house has become one large room (and a deck nearly as large) for living, reading and studying, with a pair of bedrooms flanking the entry level up top. The room is dominated by the panorama and lit by large skylights.

The main room at Hornby is a bright, gregarious social space, the site of countless dinners and parties where Kim curates the minds and personalities on a guest list, in a way that others would curate an art collection. Indeed, the couple own a few fine canvases by such esteemed Vancouver painters as Jack Shadbolt and Gordon Smith, but these are background brighteners to daily life – it is their collection of friends that is front and centre in their minds and in their conversations.

While Bo and Kim wonder about selling the Hornby house, it is hard to image this pair parting with so engaging a residence, despite its location demanding a six-hour, three-ferry *hejira* each way for weekend visits.

Their condominium in the ski resort of Whistler is a mere 100 kilometres northeast as the eagle flies, but a world apart in tone and geography. Bo worked on this very condo complex while apprenticing for Geoff Massey and Arthur Erickson, and it was built during the same era as Kim's beach house. There are few other similarities, however, as the condo is as vertical and internal as the beach house is horizontal and open to surrounding views, with bedrooms stacked on several floors up a tight spiral stair above a cozy living area – the perfect place to retreat in front of a fire after a hard day's skiing. The sources of design inspiration are evident here – the original condominium by Charles Moore of MLTW at Sea Ranch, in Northern California. The Whistler design is all angled shed roofs and greying cedar cladding, a fine exemplar of Vancouver's late 1960s domestic design tradition derived from Sea Ranch, known here alone as "Mineshaft Modern".

At the end of the 1980s, Helliwell and Smith decided to leave Hornby and relocate their practice to the city. Their first residence was a house near Horseshoe Bay designed by Barry Downs. In any other Canadian city, Downs would have been a design star, but his eminently livable house designs were eclipsed by the higher-profile work of Arthur Erickson and Ron Thom. The garage was converted into Blue Sky's studios, and the road to Whistler and first ferry to Hornby were just up the hill, easing the urban integration.

By 1998 there was a need for more room, especially for their thriving architectural practice. They also desired a location somewhat closer to the city, as volunteer activity for the local architectural lecture series plus service to professional organisations was taking more of their time. In addition, the couple's dedication to the life well lived meant increasingly regular attendance at the theatre, concerts, galleries and other exemplars of urban living located across the Lion's Gate Bridge in downtown Vancouver. The solution was a move to a second Barry Downs house closer to the city. Importantly, this second house boasted a view of that same bridge and downtown, and this symbolic connection is the final step in Helliwell and Smith's re-urbanisation.

The former John Rayer house in the Bayridge neighbourhood was designed in 1963 by Barry Downs, assisted by Fred Hollingsworth. The next year it was awarded the Massey Medal, then Canada's top award for architecture. The house is an exemplar of West Vancouver's re-working of Northwest Modernism, where purity of form is set aside for adjustments to slope and forest, where an organic palette need not be overstated, so powerful is the natural context in "completing" designs. The dominant feature of the house is its variegated roof form, which advances and withdraws from a central axis, depending on the shading needs of windows or the potential for a dramatic extension of surface and rafter into the view-plane. The house is predictive of the dominance of roof forms – what some have called "roofitecture" – in the post-1990 work of Blue Sky and their West Vancouver colleagues and friends, John and Patricia Patkau.

The Rayer house consists of two slightly splayed wings, the public rooms of kitchen dining and living canted off the axis of the bedroom wing. This deflection to landscape (this linear house runs along a site contour) yields fine harbour views on the downhill side. On the uphill or forest side there is a magnificent small garden designed by Raoul Robillard, with a carp pond and bridge near the front door, and plantings of rhododendron, cherry and Japanese maple. It is easy to see why the Rayer house and its garden attracted Helliwell and Smith, it being a small treasury of domestic design ideas. Soon, they made cosmetic changes to the interior of the house, and started planning the studio wing.

Given site contingencies and a desire to preserve and enhance the garden, there was only one location for a studio addition, along the east side of the lot, connecting with the existing house at the end of the living room. The designers decided early on that the addition would not directly extend the Downs-Hollingsworth elevational idiom, but would clearly assert itself as a Blue Sky addition, making existing house and garden look even better through creative contrast. As shown in the early design sketch by Bo, the architectural key to the studio addition came, like that of the main house, in roof design decisions. But the aesthetic here was one of contrast – the new roof would be almost completely different from that of the Rayer house. The long horizontal line of the Rayer's roof is apparent when approaching down the driveway – while the new roof sweeps up from its junction point with the existing house, making the studio's interior ceiling more visually apparent than the roof line of the original house.

The geometry of the existing Downs house is a laminate of two rectangular geometries; by contrast, the plan and structure of the new Blue Sky design studio is set out on a radial layout, and its garden-side front façade is almost completely glazed and forms an embracing part-circle in plan, turning the garden into a climate-tempered and architecturally-defined outdoor room, a frequent feature in their work. The colour palette of the existing house is light grey stucco set off with charcoal trim and grey cedar. The addition is much warmer, with a feature wall brightly painted, and otherwise the addition's exposed fir structure and oak floors glow on grey days, a counterpoint as outgoing and gregarious as the original house is serenely set unto itself. Opposite the garden, the interior wall shelters a library for design and historical monographs and material sample books, washed from above by a skylight where rafters meet the back wall. Workstations for Bo and Kim are set here, with their three or four employees set through the room closer to the glass and garden. The sum of this is one of the most sublime architectural work spaces I have ever seen, with a stunning quality of afternoon light, the sun passing through variegated trees and setting the wooden walls and appointments ablaze. Inspiration from nature and Blue Sky's organic modernist idiom enriches the work that takes place in this room. Moreover, the addition is a stunning demonstration of their design ideas, saying more about visual principles to prospective and early-days clients than any website or publication ever could.

Completed in 2000, the Bayridge architecture studio is one of Blue Sky's most significant creations – a manifesto in a room – complex in its relationships to distinct local traditions of modernism, and confident in its own course out of them. Barry Downs is now in his eighties and lives not far from Helliwell and Smith. His praise is doubtless more appreciated than anyone else's, describing the combination of his design with theirs an "imaginative complex set in the forest" that declares its architects' "commitment to organic modernism, and reverence for site and building". The most recent addition to the house is at its western end, where the bedroom has been extended and a large and light ensuite bathroom, open to views, has been added further framing Down's original with Blue Sky variations. The roof sweeps up here too, capturing but also celebrating the existing house by adding a daub of the Blue Sky palette of cedar and stone at the other end. A new downslope garden has been added, and the deck enlarged and hot tub added to make the city-side end of the Blue Sky bookend as charged with activity as the garden one.

The house and studio have become key institutions in Vancouver's architectural culture. They have been much published and broadcast as an exemplar of the continuity of organic modernist sensibilities up to the present here. They are visited constantly by architects in town for talks or consultations, and Helliwell and Smith have been generous in opening them up for regular visits by the public and architecture students. More illustration of the life well lived, every December they host a sit-down dinner for the key designers, managers, academics and yes, critic-curators, from Vancouver's architectural community. Rivals and former partners sit down together, and a sense of community rises from a very long improvised table, the dinner a rare integrative institution for a spatially and aesthetically dispersed community of architects.

Blue Sky's architecture and personalities are deeply respected, even by designers whose own predilections are radically different, and by thinkers whose taste does not tend to the organic. A social condenser for an architectural community, a workplace, a party palace, a deal closing room and an experiment in West Coast living, the Bayridge house and studio is Blue Sky's architecture at its essence.

Opposite: Blue Sky studio: current entrance and garden
Left: City gathering at home
Below: Blue Sky studio: concept drawing sketch by Bo Helliwell

Opposite: Studio entrance
Below left: Studio door detail
Below right: Entering studio

Right: Site plan
Bottom: Floor plan
Opposite top: View from entrance of studio
Opposite bottom left: Studio workspace
Opposite bottom right: Rhythm of roof rafters

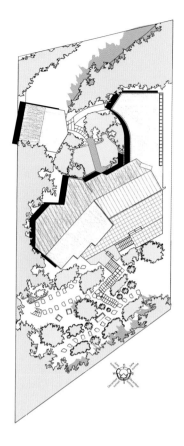

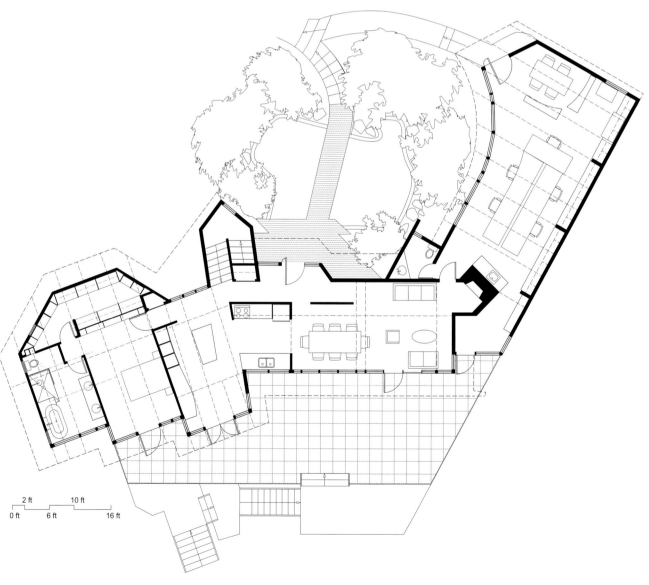

2 ft   10 ft
0 ft   6 ft   16 ft

Opposite: View towards entrance and garden
Above: View towards meeting area

Opposite: Bath with English Bay beyond
Top: Living room
Above left: Bath with redwood counter
Above right: Bedroom

A MEMETIC CONCLUSION

Let's stand back from the bucolic particular pleasures of the Bayridge to explore the broader senses of the life well lived. One of the difficulties with the concept of the life well lived is potential confusion of its principles with those tied to lifestyle marketing. When does the pleasure of occupation and life in concert with nature turn ugly – into sprawling consumption of the landscape accompanied by pointless hedonism? Is there any difference between the life well lived and the consumption cycles promoted by lifestyle marketing? In Vancouver especially, recent decades have seen the rise of sophisticated marketing for new housing, increases in height and density, and the transformation of housing from hand-crafted artifact to mass commodity.

In my view, the single most destructive notion that dulls and diminishes mass housing is the pervasive middle term of "lifestyle". It is lifestyle, not lives, that is the centre of gravity in the current housing production system – the sizzle has become the steak. Lifestyle defines the orbits of types and niches of housing, from tract houses for young families, to lofts for would-be bohemians, to recreation-retirement homes for late middle age, to care homes for the aged. To adapt housing to life-cycle stages is a good thing; to stratify populations and age groups away from each other surely is not. The fullest, richest, ripest manifestation of housing shaped around lifestyle is its advertising, not the reality as it is built. We may once have thought our cities would be shaped by the jet-cars and electric doors of science-fiction fantasy, but in fact it is the fantasies of ad-men, much more than those of scientists or architects, that shape our cities.

There is an alternative, however, to the reduction of contemporary housing to the brittle precepts of marketers, and the convenient shorthand of lifestyle. If housing is not to be structured around ideas of lifestyle, what then, could take its place? There is perhaps no finer ambition for our dwellings than for them to be the means to achieve "The life well lived". Can the forms and textures of a house both exemplify the lives of its owners, and allow them to deepen and enrich that life? Not an icon, not a status symbol, not the ritual possessions of the wealthy, but can a house become an instrument of living well?

Answers for many of these questions can be found in the houses assembled here designed by Kim Smith and Bo Helliwell. I have toured these houses and have listened to and observed their clients. As occupied houses, these nearly always second or seasonal homes boast the physical evidence of the books, clothes, furniture and art that is arrayed within them. The evidence I have found in the voices and artifacts of these owners is nearly always the same: "With this house I will improve my life. With these walls I will integrate my values. With this retreat I will attain that which has become separated from me".

Blue Sky Architecture does very little promotion other than to collect design awards and to collaborate on the 1998 book I edited for them, also for Images Publishing (*Picturesque, Tectonic, Romantic: Helliwell + Smith, Blue Sky Architecture*) and a few magazine articles. In the absence of conventional marketing, their most important instrument of engagement is, of course, the magnetic attractiveness of the houses themselves. They are strange enough in form and shape to attract attention at even the initial stage of staking the site, yet so warmly inhabitable at completion to have seemed inevitable and effortless. The houses attract curiosity (always the sign of originality), but mature upon repeated viewings and visits without the strange-making that too many architects confuse with creativity.

If one steps back from architecture, to what degree is this notion of "The life well lived" part of Vancouver's urban culture? Or is it just a bourgeois eccentricity exiled to its leafy suburbs or mountainous hinterland? While editing this volume, I have also been writing a book on Vancouver architecture and city-building, based on my exhibition "Vancouverism: Architecture Builds the City", which was shown between 2008–2010 in London, Paris and here in Vancouver. In trying to explain Vancouver to the world, I have been writing about how our city fares better at exporting viral-like ideas, or memes, than it does producing manufactured goods or providing homes to large corporations. For a city its size, Vancouver has precious little manufacturing, and its greatest success has come in the past two decades, when it has evolved a virtual single-industry economy based on real estate. At the core of this industry is a concern for quality of life, if one accepts it positively, or the shameless marketing of lifestyle, if one tends more to criticism. In trying to determine which side of the line is home to the life well lived – the essence of quality of life, or the material expression of lifestyle marketing – some powerful Vancouver-generated cultural memes (viral ideas that spread globally) tell us something interesting.

First, I'll give a quick introduction to some of these Vancouver-generated global memes. To start, consider the activist environmental organisation, exemplified in the founding of Greenpeace here in the early 1970s. Next is Vancouver novelist William Gibson's naming of the pervasive environment of information in a short story, then the 1983 novel *Neuromancer*. Back then he called it "cyberspace", and now we all do. Next up is another novelist, who is also a public artist and student and collector of Mid-Century modernism, who lives in West Vancouver near Helliwell and Smith. Douglas Coupland has named one generation globally "Generation X", and implied the naming of another with its evolution into "Generation Y". While there are others, the most recent and high-profile of Vancouver-created memes is the "Occupy" movement, whose manifesto was posted online 13 July 2011 by a Vancouver-based group at *Adbusters* magazine, including editor Kalle Lasn.

Our city has few corporate head offices, does not create globally desired services like Seattle's Microsoft and Amazon, was never home base to exporting factories of consequence, but despite all this, our memes regularly broadcast out to change thinking elsewhere. What links these memes is a brutal honesty about the nature of the world past the mediated surfaces of lifestyle (Cyberspace, Generation X), or the creation of movements hoping to shape a greener, more equitable society (Greenpeace, Occupy). In other words, Vancouver is a generator of Blue Sky thinking. Is it a coincidence that this firm, founded amid the counter-cultural wood butchers of Hornby Island in the early 1970s, has now come to occupy a position closer to the centre of Vancouver's urban life? Vancouver produces memes telling us ways to understand and master the life well lived, and now it seems we also have architects with the same message.

Vancouver 2012

Trevor Boddy, BA M.Arch. MRAIC AIA Hon.

Vancouver-based Trevor Boddy is an architecture critic, commentator on urbanism and city-building and consulting urban designer. He has received the Alberta Book of the Year Prize, Jack Webster Journalism Prize, *Western Magazine* Award, named Honorary Member of the American Institute of Architects, and the Royal Architectural Institute of Canada's 2010 Advocacy Award for his writing on buildings and cities. At the 2011 World Congress of Architecture in Tokyo, Boddy's essay (for *AV* in Madrid) on contemporary design in his country entitled "MEGA + MICRO: Canada, Innovation at the Extremes" was awarded a commendation for the UIA's Pierre Vago Prize as the best piece of architectural criticism published worldwide in the preceding three years. As a consulting urban designer, he has co-devised architectural competitions including Surrey's "TownShift: Suburb Into City" (www.townshift.ca). His "HybridCity" was included in Vancouver Art Gallery's 2011 exhibition "WE Vancouver: 12 Manifestos for the City". As architectural curator, Trevor produced the "Vancouverism: Architecture Builds the City" exhibition in 2008 and related Trafalgar Square site-specific construction, named a marquee event for the 2008 London Festival of Architecture, remounted it in Paris in 2009, then brought it back to Vancouver for the 2010 Winter Olympic Games.

BLUE SKY THINKING

Nature and culture are deeply intertwined with the shape of building designs. This is especially true in the naturally blessed, culturally rich corner of the world where we live and practise architecture. We have developed a way of building that is rooted in place, inspired by curiosity, responsive to natural forces and which seeks physical, emotional and spiritual connections between people and places.

1 **SEEK SITE GUIDANCE FOR SENSE OF PLACE** Let the lines of the land guide building forms in both plan and section; let buildings flex their walls to follow, not dominate the fluid lines of landscape; let the buildings amplify the beauty, knowledge and sense of place of their sites.

2 **CAPTURE LIGHT** Natural light animates, warms and enlivens architecture. In the often grey-skied backdrop of the Pacific Northwest, it is even more essential to bring natural light into all spaces. Natural light acts as a timekeeper in buildings, connecting us to the passing of the day, progress of the seasons, and status of weather. Natural light must be tempered and balanced to avoid glare, so that eastern light is balanced with western; and indirect northern light tempered with bright highlights from the south.

3 **SHAPE ORGANIC FORMS** There are very few straight lines and square boxes in nature. By designing with fluid and non-linear forms, our buildings integrate with landscapes and produce sensual and embracing spaces, breaking down barriers between environment and built form.

4 **STRUCTURE SPACE** Whenever possible, expose key structural elements, as their presence teaches inhabitants the forces on their dwellings, and helps make sense of the spaces they frame. Beams project through space and rafters dance up and down to turn simple roofs into sculptures. This directness in structural expression means what you see and feel is real. Modulating structure can vary the feeling of space, shifting between surprise and embrace, movement and rest, fluid and static, expansion and compression.

5 **SUPPLEMENT SHELTER** With a temperate climate, outdoor rooms (large sheltered spaces) create year-round opportunities to be outside in comfortably contemplative ways, sheltered from rain, wind and sun.

6 **CELEBRATE WEATHER** For our temperate rainforest climate, we build large, simple sheltering roofs. We celebrate rather than resist the rain, forming roofs to gather, direct, and store rainwater for re-use inside and for landscaping uses outside.

7 **USE NATURAL MATERIALS AND COLOUR** Use palettes of natural materials where possible, and avoid those that deposit toxins. The neutral and subtle colours of wood and stone provide buildings with warmth and connectedness to place. These are living, haptic qualities that no synthetic material can emulate. This said, occasional highlights of bright colour works as punctuation, playfully emphasising rhythm and texture.

8 **CRAFT** The use of fine craft to shape unique objects adds value, care and personality to a building. The sense of pride resulting from fine building craftsmanship builds spatial legacies that never fade.

9 **USE NATURAL ENERGY** Utilise natural energy available on site, including sun, wind, geo-thermal and water. Design and build to conserve material use and energy consumption. Shape building sections to allow natural light to illuminate rooms and natural convection currents to ventilate them.

10 **SEIZE OPPORTUNITIES** During the course of construction, opportunities appear as materials are connected and spaces formed. An unexpected sightline may emerge, a beautiful boulder discovered during site preparation – notice and take advantage of these opportunities.

Kim Smith and Bo Helliwell
West Vancouver/Whistler/Hornby

Opposite: Hill House: Hillside terrace and islands beyond

BLUE SKY LIVING: THE PROJECTS

This volume was preceded by a 1998 publication – also produced in association with Images Publishing, and also edited by Trevor Boddy – entitled *Picturesque, Tectonic, Romantic: Helliwell + Smith, Blue Sky Architecture*. Five houses from that book are included here; the other houses on these pages were completed since 2000, and now include multi-family housing and public buildings, as well as single-family residences. Reviewing and organising 30 years of work has revealed a number of thematic threads that weave together our evolving body of work. While each of these designs arises out of its own site considerations, budget and brief contingencies, and the inspirations of client and design team, we have grouped them with fellow-travelling designs into a sequence of chapters. All of the projects have their own inspirations and problems to solve and are approached with the principles of Blue Sky Thinking; some lean more heavily towards one conceptual framework than others. Accordingly, we have organized the projects in this book into these six chapter headings:

NARRATIVE For some designs, a poetic story motivates its creative forms and connections. These might be a passion for the land or a personal passion by the owner that sparks an image or metaphor. Whether this is fish, comet or library, they are used as design devices to shape the visible form, material and structure of the final building.

PLACE All sites have design-informing character, but for some locations' spirit of place is so powerful that it obliges buildings to become a direct extension of the land. In many of our sites in the North American west, there is extreme topography, or nature in its rawest form, or vistas beyond description. Blue Sky designs buildings that sit or walk lightly upon the land.

STRUCTURE We work primarily in wood and express the power, beauty and life of timber by revealing and celebrating the structure of the building. Sometimes the geometry and proportion of timber structures is the primary character-defining element in the design.

TECTONIC Blue Sky's designs seek to reveal the tactility and beauty of materials through celebrating fine craft and details – in connections are found the essence of building. We often incorporate found or treasured and recycled building parts that become embedded and celebrated in surrounding new constructions.

SYSTEMS We work with passive and active energy systems for buildings and construction operations. Often our buildings are not connected to urban services and are independent for water, waste and energy systems. In other cases their energy and water systems are enhanced through geo-exchange, passive design and water conservation systems designed into the buildings.

COMMUNITY All of our buildings contribute to communities of people, starting with families and friends, to neighbourhoods and cities. Some projects stand individually and others are planned communities – all seek to become part of a greater whole, and to give back in either beauty, public amenity or both.

Opposite: Main hall of Oak Grove House

BOOKLOVERS' HOUSE

NARRATIVE

Sidney Island, British Columbia
250 sq. m. (2700 sq. ft)
2004–2008

The owners are Prairie bookstore operators who fell in love with Sidney Island, and now spend their summers in this remote 'library in the woods'. Books are a passion and not just a vocation for the couple, as they are avid readers and active book collectors. Their literary sensibilities have inspired and tempered the blend of formal and bookish references for their home's design.

The site is seafront on a small island in the Strait of Juan de Fuca, between Vancouver Island and the San Juan Islands, with no ferry access or local services. The house is off-grid and situated on a point of shoreline facing northeast. This sets up a tension in devising a plan between orientating towards ocean views to the north and sunshine to the south. The home and garden carve out a readerly refuge in this wild location, combining a geometrically formal overall plan with organic and sensuous elements – a library with nooks, not just books. In plan, the house and walled garden complex is an oval intersected with an axis directed towards a small point on the shoreline. In section, the greater upper roof curves to orient to the sun and to form a hierarchy of spaces. Lower flat roofs allow for optimal placement of solar panels, while maximising natural ventilation and light penetration into the heart of the house. Walls are largely transparent, facing the central garden spaces. Sunshine penetrates deep into interior spaces, while on the other side, the expanse of ocean is visible from all rooms.

The island has a very large wild deer population and all gardens need high fencing to protect plants flowers and trees. The fenced oval creates a formal cloistered space, a south-facing outdoor room that shelters the intensively planted inner garden. Two garden tool sheds form a gateway into the garden room. A main entry to the house intersects a gallery-corridor lined with rows of open bookshelves, mounted between structural fir posts, dividing entrance and hallway from the great room.

Top: Model – south view
Right: Axial view from entry across garden
Opposite top left: Site plan
Opposite top right: Exterior view to point

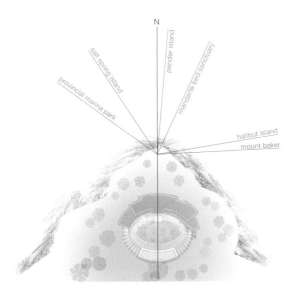

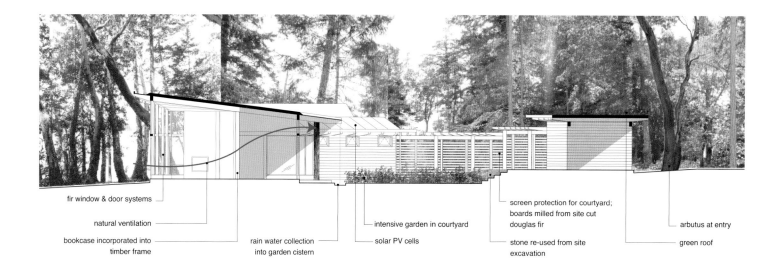

fir window & door systems

natural ventilation

bookcase incorporated into
timber frame

rain water collection
into garden cistern

solar PV cells

intensive garden in courtyard

screen protection for courtyard;
boards milled from site cut
douglas fir

stone re-used from site
excavation

arbutus at entry

green roof

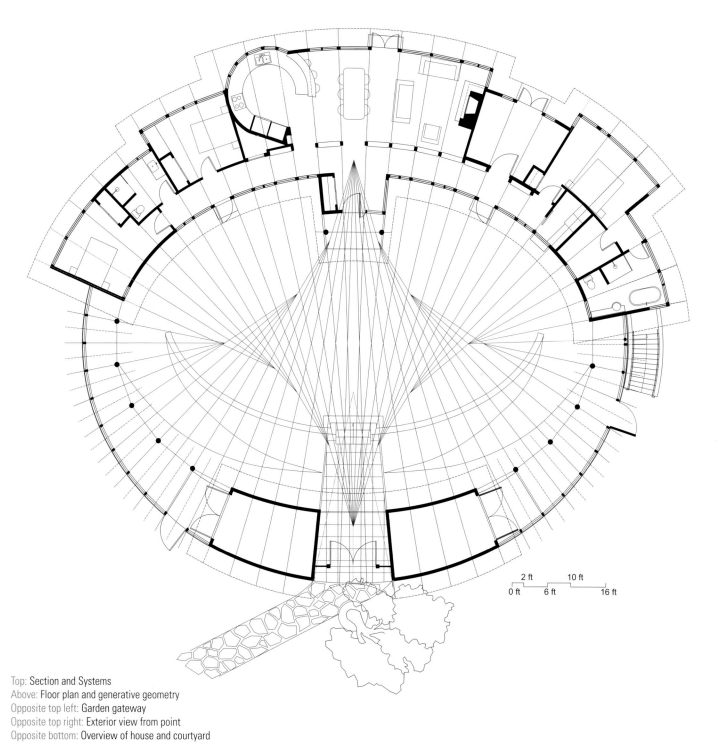

2 ft   10 ft
0 ft   6 ft   16 ft

Top: Section and Systems
Above: Floor plan and generative geometry
Opposite top left: Garden gateway
Opposite top right: Exterior view from point
Opposite bottom: Overview of house and courtyard

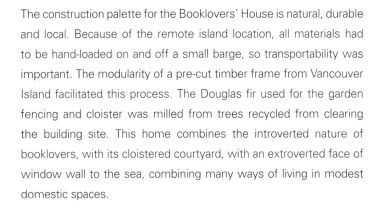

The construction palette for the Booklovers' House is natural, durable and local. Because of the remote island location, all materials had to be hand-loaded on and off a small barge, so transportability was important. The modularity of a pre-cut timber frame from Vancouver Island facilitated this process. The Douglas fir used for the garden fencing and cloister was milled from trees recycled from clearing the building site. This home combines the introverted nature of booklovers, with its cloistered courtyard, with an extroverted face of window wall to the sea, combining many ways of living in modest domestic spaces.

Below left and opposite: Hallway/library
Below right: Living and dining room
Bottom: Kitchen
Following pages: Dining and kitchen

COMET HOUSE

NARRATIVE

Colorado, USA
186 sq. m. (2000 sq. ft)
2000–2005

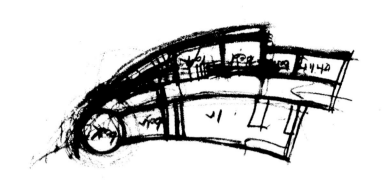

Comet House is an optimistic and romantic endeavour. The design of the house is driven by its owners' passion for stars, sun and the raw landscapes of Northern Colorado's high-altitude rangelands. The house serves as a culmination for a life in amateur astronomy along with an appreciation for the dramatic western landscape. She is a photographer and film-maker impassioned by the land and light; he is a serious amateur astronomer wanting to watch the stars visible in the exceptionally dark skies available there. Via the internet, a domed observatory roof can be opened and rotated by remote control and a high-powered 18-inch-diameter telescope manipulated to watch the stars on a computer screen anywhere. All this is possible without telecom wires or links to the power grid, as the house is entirely solar powered and connected to the world via satellite up-link.

One of the unusual design challenges for this house is that it is thus occupied at various times physically from Colorado, or virtually from Connecticut. The design metaphor of the comet manifests in many of the house's features: plan-forms radiate out from the head-like, round geometry of the observatory dome; tail-like walls flow outwards to embrace the natural lines of the site; distant views of the Rocky Mountains are captured and framed by the unexpected event of this building. Low sloping and gently curving roof forms echo the grassy hills around the building. Inside, an undulating structure is shaped from exposed fir beams/rafters. Along these curving walls, window mullions double as structural supports for the timber frame. The site brought its own demands to construction choices. Strict local requirements mandated little or no change to landscapes visible from neighbouring house sites. An encircling stone base protects the house from the area's periodic grassfires. A remote site and the seasonal use pattern mean this house must operate self-sufficiently much of the year. A solar panel array and windmill with a back-up propane generator guarantee a continuous

Top: Concept sketch plan
Right: Southeast elevation at night

energy supply for its sophisticated communication systems. Inside, two platforms rise up to the observatory. One supports a library, the other an office/control room. These raised platforms lend a dramatic and theatrical ambience to the main spaces of the house. The raked geometry of the north elevation and the stairs to the observatory evoke Helliwell and Smith's admiration for the Jantar Mantar, the 18th-century astronomical instrument-cum-buildings they toured near Jaipur, India. The observatory dome of Comet House is the only object visible from the surrounding hills. The celestial engagement of the observatory fuses into an alternate reading of this house as an agricultural building – from the plough to the stars!

A circular sitting room below the observatory features two independent concrete columns aligned precisely north–south supporting a large steel beam, where the telescope is fixed above. This portal frame is insulated from the house's own structure to ensure that thermal differences and vibrations do not compromise the telescope's performance. Alluding to scientific and mathematical experiments from the Renaissance, and extending the house's other celestial metaphors, a precisely formed slot was cast in the south column and a brass strip was inlaid in the floor forming a Meridiana (meridian line) that tracks the seasonal sun shift at solar high noon. The design of Comet House is a fusion of site contingencies, scientific requirements and a playfully poetic design interpretation. It reflects the cyclical interplay between the earth and sky – a temporal bridge connecting celestial observation and terrestrial occupation – sun and wind-powered to create a portal to the cosmos.

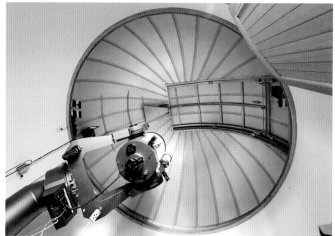

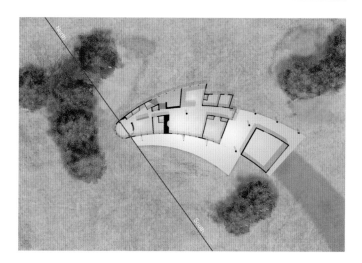

Top: South elevation
Middle: Observatory
Right: Site plan
Opposite bottom: View from northeast

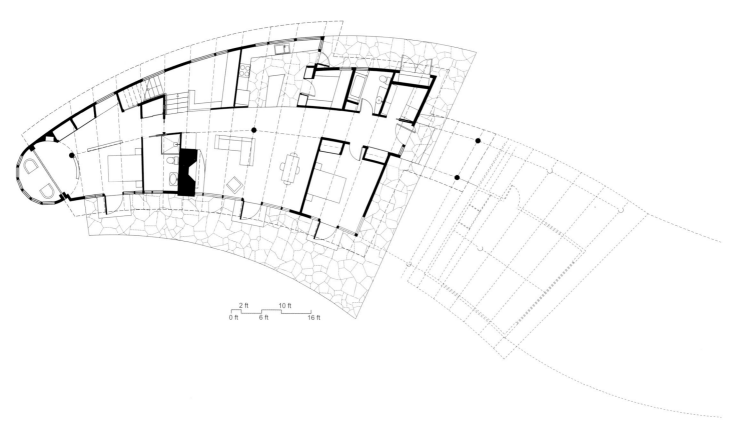

Opposite top: Floor plan
Opposite bottom: Looking towards living and library
Left: Great room from library
Below: Section and Systems

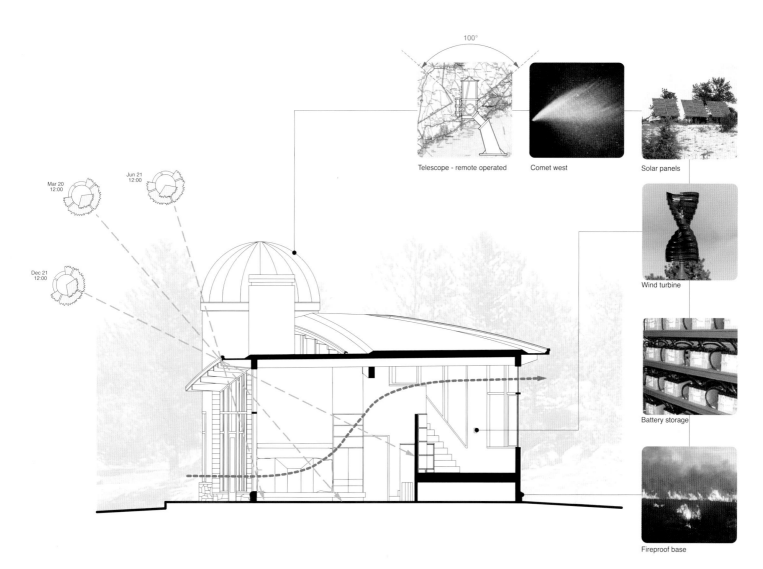

100°

Telescope - remote operated

Comet west

Solar panels

Wind turbine

Battery storage

Fireproof base

Mar 20 12:00

Jun 21 12:00

Dec 21 12:00

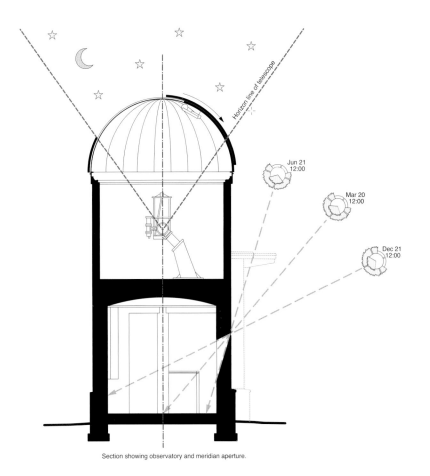

Section showing observatory and meridian aperture.

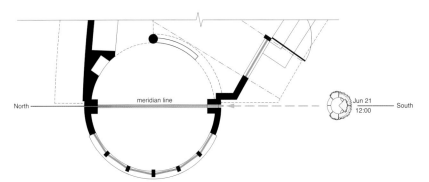

Plan of meridian room (observatory above)

North — meridian line — South

Opposite top left: Observatory and meridian room details
Opposite bottom left: Meridian room
Opposite bottom right: Master bedroom
Above: Great room

UCLUELET AQUARIUM

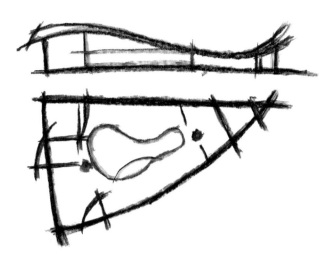

NARRATIVE
Ucluelet, Vancouver Island, British Columbia
492.5 sq. m. (5300 sq. ft)
2008–2012

The Ucluelet Aquarium is a teaching environment, a creation of community effort and imagination, and a waterfront gathering place at the centre of town. This teaching building is conceived and built by local residents, its purpose being the sharing of information about the ocean, and the integrated nature of seas with land and air ecosystems. The entire project was initiated by Ucluelet area residents, and sustained with their donations of time, money and material. Only later was this supplemented by government grants once the project attained a momentum that was evident to all.

Given its community provenance, it is no surprise that the layout and features of Ucluelet's Aquarium signal a significant departure from conventional aquarium designs. Instead of splitting the building into behind-the-scenes and public areas, this aquarium invites visitors to participate in and to observe all day-to-day support and preparation activities. In traditional aquariums, many of the most interesting and essential activities (preparation of feedings, testing of the health of fish, research, etc.) happen away from visitors' eyes. Not here. Blue Sky's architectural conception encourages visitors and staff to engage

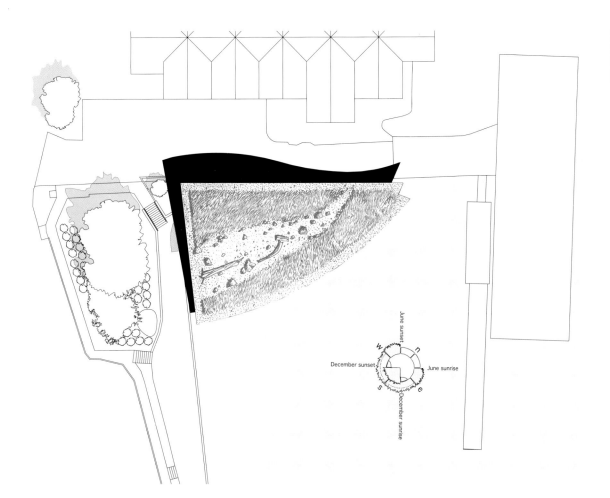

Opposite top: Concept sketch
Opposite bottom: Harbour view
Right: Site plan
Bottom: Entrance

June sunset
December sunset
June sunrise
December sunrise

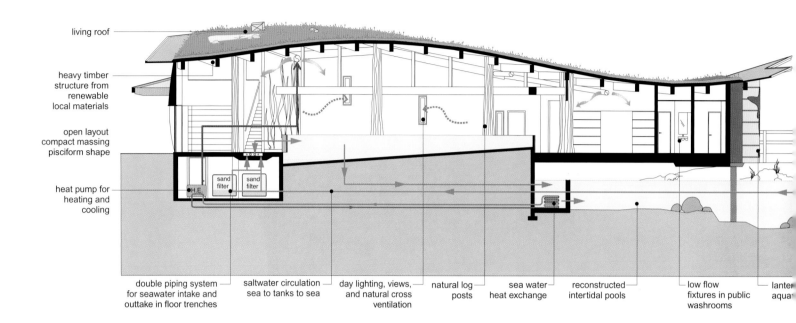

living roof

heavy timber
structure from
renewable
local materials

open layout
compact massing
pisciform shape

heat pump for
heating and
cooling

sand filter   sand filter   H.E

double piping system
for seawater intake and
outtake in floor trenches

saltwater circulation
sea to tanks to sea

day lighting, views,
and natural cross
ventilation

natural log
posts

sea water
heat exchange

reconstructed
intertidal pools

low flow
fixtures in public
washrooms

lanter
aqua

on common ground; the layout encouraging impromptu events and encounters throughout this 'non-zoned' building. Easy observations of movement, feeding, and mating by marine life are used to launch a highly intimate dialogue between the natural and human worlds. Display tanks are sized to allow visitors and staff direct physical contact with those sea-life specimens that are able to tolerate or even thrive from such interactions. Being able to feel, smell or hear marine life creates memorable experiences that then become associated with the aquarium's natural history and conservation agenda.

Architectural elements combine to foster understanding of marine environments. These include maritime-inspired design motifs throughout the building; local beach grasses and gravel installed on the green roof; the intertidal zone visible and interpreted underneath the building; and inside, the marine displays themselves. The shape of the building is fish-like, with two land-facing walls featuring fish graphics. The building is laid out around a central saltwater pool providing views of local marine life. This main pool and smaller aquarium tanks are all interconnected by water channels and valves that distribute salt water from the inlet and return it through a heat-exchange unit. The marine animals on display here are temporarily 'borrowed' from local seas, displayed for short periods, and then returned to their local habitats. A large glazed wall on the east side of the building visually connects the aquarium's interior to the harbour. Opening windows there and on the west wall enables natural ventilation. The dramatic timber post-and-beam structure was sourced from trees in nearby forests and donated by the local saw-mill.

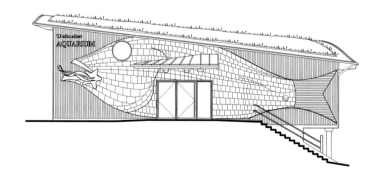

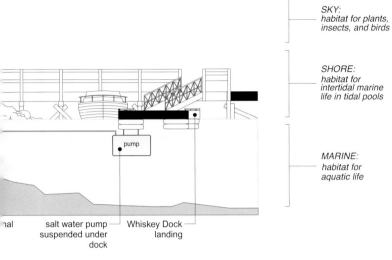

SKY:
habitat for plants, insects, and birds

SHORE:
habitat for intertidal marine life in tidal pools

MARINE:
habitat for aquatic life

nal
salt water pump
suspended under
dock

Whiskey Dock
landing

pump

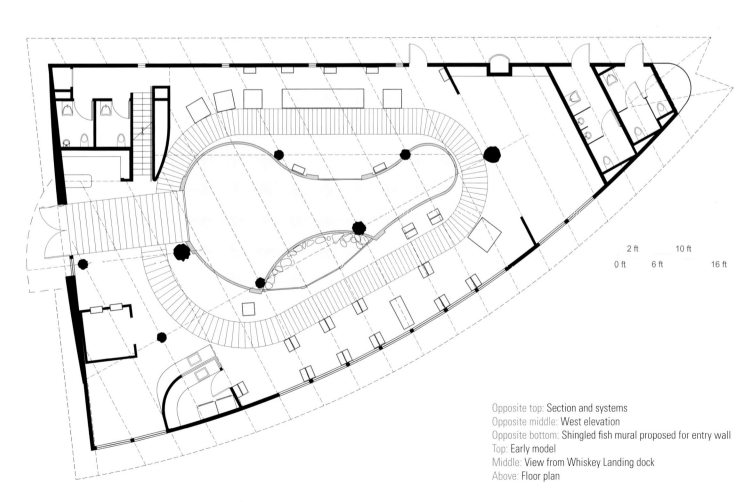

2 ft   10 ft
0 ft   6 ft   16 ft

Opposite top: Section and systems
Opposite middle: West elevation
Opposite bottom: Shingled fish mural proposed for entry wall
Top: Early model
Middle: View from Whiskey Landing dock
Above: Floor plan

Plans and building material efficiencies make this aquarium modest and sustainable, while also reducing volunteer oversight requirements. Supporting the sea-life displays, the Aquarium contains an entrance foyer/gathering place, gift shop, office space, a children's activity area and a lecture hall/marine biology research area. There are also public washrooms accessible from the main public dock, a community amenity for all. Display tanks have been recycled from other public aquariums; renewable locally sourced wood is the primary structural building material; the floor is an efficient and low-maintenance concrete slab resting on top of concrete beams and pilings. Ingenuity in design and display construction effectively increases – not diminishes – the area of active fish and shore habitat that existed there in its previous state. With its innovative and community-responsive exhibition philosophy and design, the Ucluelet Aquarium invites nature to reclaim many of its spaces. The iconic shape of the 'pisci-form' roof supports an extensive planted area that will become home to native plants, insects, and even

Top: Night view from Whiskey Landing dock
Right: Tidal pool
Opposite top: View from kids' area
Opposite bottom: Tidal pool action
Following pages: Tidal pool and library

nesting birds. The main exhibit level is thus a small but biologically productive extension of the Pacific Ocean. By building the aquarium on a suspended slab, the aquarium preserves the existing shore, which has been turned into intertidal garden pools with water and rock features that are supplemented by seawater recycling from the displays above. The intertidal garden is part of an extension of the aquarium out into the marine ecosystem. The building is similarly an extension of the social life of the town of Ucluelet. The boundary between nature and aquarium is creatively blurred because Blue Sky's architecture crafts connections, both natural and human.

Top: View from entrance
Middle: Concept rendering of interior
Bottom: View from library
Opposite: Tidal walkway and service trench

HARBOUR HOUSE

PLACE   Eagle Harbour, West Vancouver, British Columbia
372 sq. m. (4000 sq. ft)
2004–2008

Eagle Harbour is a south-facing bay not far from the Helliwell/Smith office in West Vancouver. The site here was almost impossible to build yet visually spectacular – a solid granite cliff set just above a protected, yacht-filled harbour. This house is conceived as an extension of existing topographic lines, producing an architecture of dynamic curved walls and flying roofs sweeping across a rock face.

The house's massing steps back from the road as it rises up the cliff. Each floor level is narrow in depth, elongated and stretched in a curved geometry following the cliff's topography. Split level planning helps minimize vertical circulation throughout the house. In order to reduce visual impact at this high-profile location, care has been taken with roof shapes and details. Low-rise curving roof profiles reduce perceived building height and open interiors to natural light and harbour views.

Exposed Douglas fir laminated beams and rafters curve above interiors, sculpting their spaces. Complementing its rocky cliff setting, an expressed timber frame and clear red cedar siding provide natural textures. A terrace is formed over the driveway by an extreme cantilever of large laminated beams. This partially covered south-facing terrace allows for outdoor living in most weather conditions, with large overhangs protecting from extremes of rain and sun.

The house has a nautical feel in its detailing; the curving cedar walls echo hulls of sailboats floating in nearby Eagle Harbour. Fair-faced concrete retaining walls for the driveway, entrance stairs and the foundation reinforce the lines of the site and architecture. Granite quarried from the site is used in the landscaping. Harbour House builds on the tradition of West Coast modernism, with a bold structure and warm material palette inspired by a dramatic natural setting.

Top: Model view
Right: View from southwest
Opposite top: Site plan

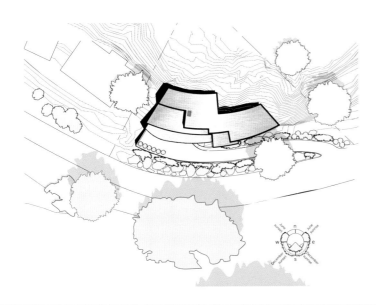

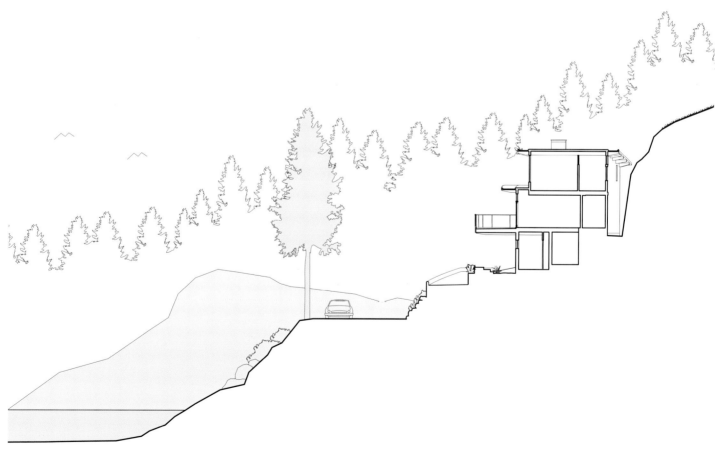

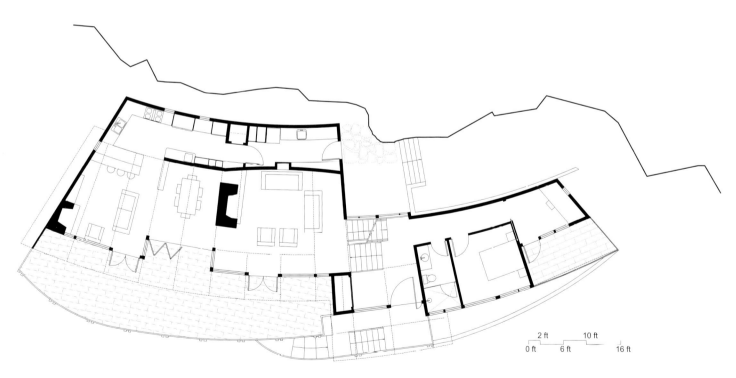

Opposite top: View from street
Opposite bottom: Site section
Top left: Relationship of house to cliff
Top right: Stair with view of cliff
Above: Floor plan

Left: Living room
Opposite bottom left: Roof detail
Opposite bottom right: Relationship of house to harbour and cliff
Below: Terrace
Bottom: Staircase

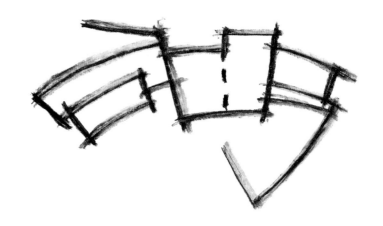

HILL HOUSE

Salt Spring Island, British Columbia
483 sq. m. (5200 sq. ft)
2000–2003

This is the first of a series of homes designed and built on Salt Spring Island since 2000. The site on Mount Tuam is a moss-covered rocky ridge, 200 metres (655 feet) above Satellite Channel. View lines from the site sweep from vistas of Vancouver to the northeast, while to the south and west is the pastoral Saanich Peninsula and the Southern Gulf and San Juan Islands. The house is oriented to the southeast, to embrace light and expansive views over the Gulf. Hill House is approached through a cool, shaded forest. Rough topography prompts an organic, curving plan that threads along a spine of exposed rocks. The design overhangs the ridge in some places while in others it nestles back into the hillside. The lower floor has been inserted into a niche in the rocks and its roof built out to form a large outdoor terrace above, thus creating the only readily adjacent outdoor space.

This house commences a decade's string of collaborations with builder Gord Speed, a skilled, careful and creative craftsman who served as an apprentice under acclaimed Salt Spring Island architect Hank Schubart. Speed brought an intelligent curiosity and an aptitude for innovating in construction and materials. Among many details developed with Speed is Blue Sky's recurring wall-cladding system, comprising three clear cedar horizontal siding boards spaced with a horizontal copper strip. The copper strips are given a reddish patina through application of a gentle acid bath of apple cider vinegar.

An open and fluid approach to the design and construction prompted other innovations in materials and techniques. For example, a solid piece of sandstone 1.2 metres by 2.25 metres by 3 metres (4 feet by 7 feet 6 inches by 10 feet) from Salt Spring Island was used as a vertical accent to the large Rumford fireplace. Similarly, a singular piece of basalt from local mountains was drilled and formed as a one-piece sink and counter. Another innovation in detail were the two sets of oversized sliding doors, one set 2.4 metres by 2.75 metres (8 feet

Top: Concept sketch
Right: View of south terrace
Opposite top left: Site plan
Opposite top right: Digital rendering of roof structure

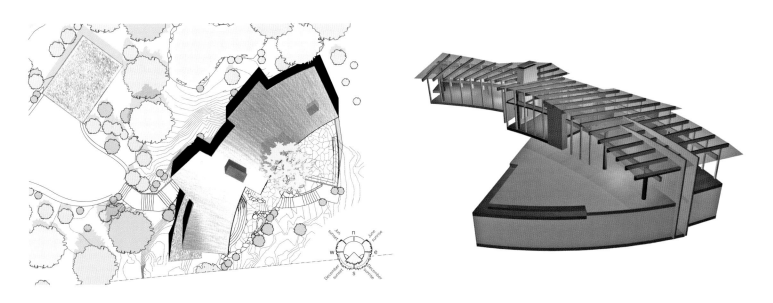

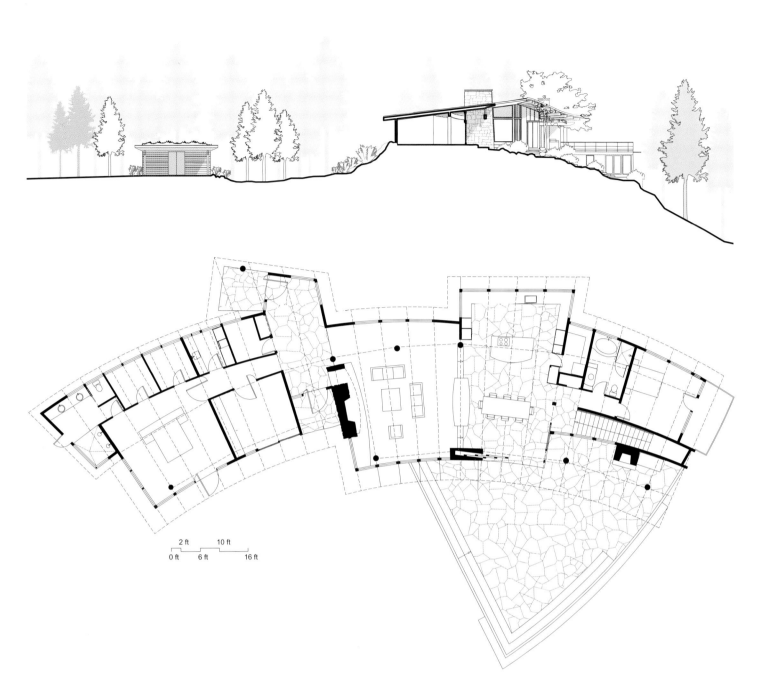

2 ft   10 ft
0 ft   6 ft   16 ft

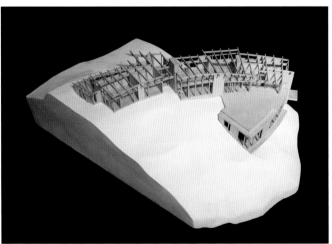

by 9 feet) and one set 3.65 metres by 2.25 metres (12 feet by 7 feet 6 inches). These combine to shape an unobstructed opening corner, with recessed track and drain, making for a seamless transition between house interior and terrace/views outside.

Pivotal in Blue Sky's design development, this house is larger in programme and budget than previous commissions. This allowed an experimental and collaborative approach to building systems and materials. With Hill House, Blue Sky continues a design evolution away from simple Euclidian geometric planning into more natural, flowing and organic house layouts and site planning. The topography of this Salt Spring site, with its rocky ridge, precipitates a residence that seems to evolve naturally out of it, the landscape extended in wood and glass.

Opposite top: South elevation
Opposite bottom: View of entry from west
Top: Section
Middle: Floor plan
Bottom: Model photo

Opposite: Living
Top: Living and dining
Left: Sandstone slab at fireplace
Above left: Stair space
Above right: Detail of cedar and copper wall cladding

RIDGE HOUSE

PLACE

Salt Spring Island, British Columbia
288 sq. m. (3100 sq. ft)
2003–2007

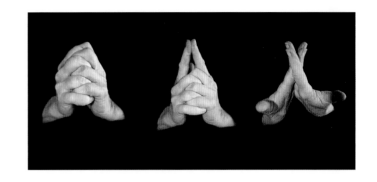

This house's structure resembles the laced-fingered children's game of "Here's the church, here's the steeple, open the doors to see all the people". The rhythm of the roof inflects the 'spatial moods' of rooms below, as it shifts from the entrance's enclosed and protective forms, to open and expansive spaces for the living and dining rooms. Above the entrance, the roof shapes a gable-dominated elevation. Rooms are all accessed off a central hallway that is aligned with the roof ridge's centerline. This central hall expands in width as it moves toward the views. As one passes through the house, exposed rafters gradually invert a gable roof into a butterfly roof, setting back to form an opening that integrates light and views into key social areas.

The house is the embodiment of its owners' retirement dreams. Having owned and camped out at this heavily treed, steep hillside site for several years, they had time to formulate their ideas for living here. Selecting their preferred building site, the couple had identified

Top: **Here's the church; Here's the steeple; Here's the people**
Right: **View from northwest**
Below: **Site plan**
Opposite top left: **View of model**
Opposite top right: **View from main entrance**

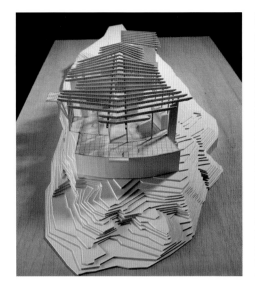

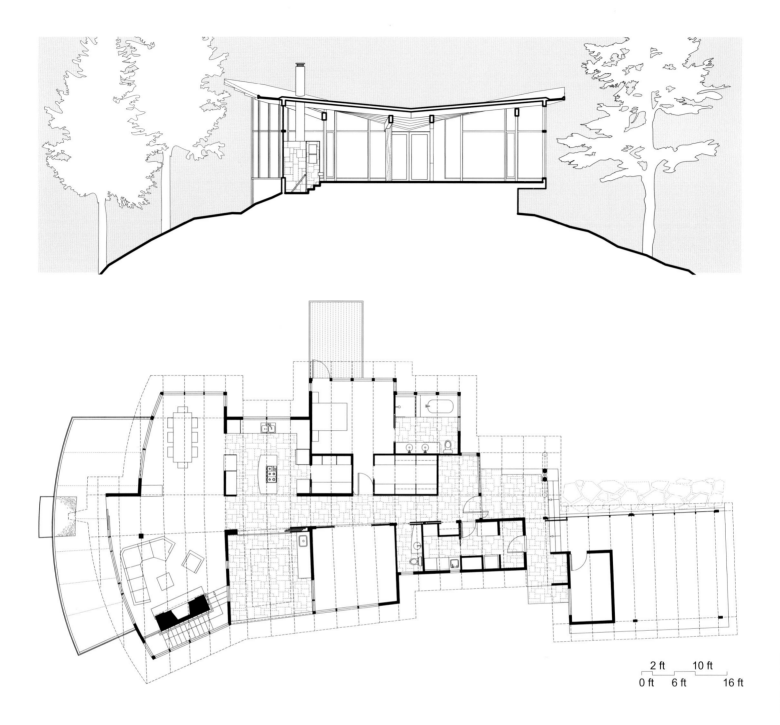

2 ft   10 ft

0 ft   6 ft   16 ft

a narrow rocky ridge, running approximately east–west through a grove of small twisted arbutus trees. The Ridge House's linear plan and section are determined by this topography. Most rooms are set on one level: living room, dining room, kitchen, den and main bedroom suite. Adjacent to the master bedroom is a bird-watching deck that projects north into the treetops. A covered outdoor room opens onto the arbutus grove to the south, providing a sheltered all-season outdoor living space. At the west end of the house where the property drops away, there is a lower floor guest suite, office area and wine cellar, all below the terrace above.

Rainwater from the butterfly roof is channeled into an exaggerated scupper, which funnels water into a pond set into the main terrace. This pond is centered on the house's central hall and, when full of

water, serves as a small reflecting pond that both terminates and visually extends the axis. Roof water is collected in cisterns and used for site irrigation. Passive heating is assisted by a south-facing stairwell window wall and the thermal mass of the masonry fireplace wall. The structure is a simply expressed Douglas fir post-and-beam, but the elevations are complex and differentiated on each side. Door and window systems are designed to be integral with this timber frame structure. Each window mullion is a structural Douglas fir post supporting rafters and decking. The rafters balance on two ridge beams that run axially through the space, their varied slopes forming a wave to create sculpted spaces. Simple details and careful craftsmanship aggregate to form a sophisticated design that perches dramatically on its rocky forest ridge.

Opposite top: Section
Opposite bottom: Floor plan
Top: View from west
Left: Front entrance
Above: Post base detail

Left: Living area
Top: South-facing stair and fireplace wall
Above: Handrail detail

Opposite: View towards entrance
Left: Roof rainwater scupper and pond
Below: Dining

MIRACLE BEACH HOUSE

STRUCTURE

Vancouver Island, British Columbia
627 sq. m. (6750 sq. ft)
2004–2008

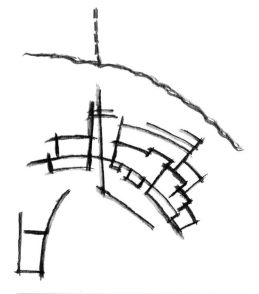

Structure and spatial simplicity are the responses to the power of this bracing seaside site, revealing it in both subtle and majestic ways. A grand pebbled crescent, Miracle Beach is dominated by startling vistas across Georgia Strait to snow-capped mountains on the mainland. This compound of house, studio and garage forms a convex curve, which is set in opposition to the concave curve of the beach. The two curves inspire a sheltered courtyard that captures the southern sun on the forest side of the plan. The house's structure is a mix of fir timber frames anchored by large concrete shear columns. The exterior finish palette is bluestone, glass, red cedar and feature walls with brightly coloured glass tiles.

The home was conceived as a gathering place for an extended family dividing their time between England and Vancouver Island. A transparent hallway with opening walls invokes the notion of two linked homes – one for the teenagers and the other for their parents. Many of the glass walls of the house use convertible frames, allowing them to pivot from windows into doors. Twelve metres (40 feet) of hallway walls use folding accordion doors, while another series of 1.5 metre by 2.75 metre (5 feet by 9 feet) doors pivot open on the sea side of the main social spaces, making for a dwelling that can almost completely open out into its setting.

Exposed curving laminated beams modulate interior spaces, highlighting the circulation spine and instilling in visitors a sense of curiosity for what lies beyond. An unusually bold example of an evolving Blue Sky structural/spatial strategy, these beams support a series of undulating rafters, their variation shaping sensual, sculptural spaces. The curving beams are set onto vertical concrete fins – oversized vertical anchors that provide a sense of gravitas and tectonic syntax. All shear structural forces are resolved into these cast concrete monoliths, exposed on the inside and clad in large bluestone slabs outside. The arcs in plan continue around as a unifying

Top: Concept sketch
Right: View from beach
Opposite top: Section

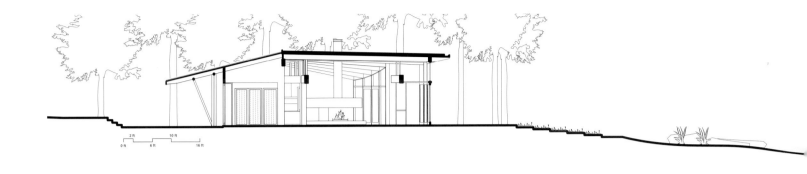

2 ft
10 ft
0 ft
6 ft
16 ft

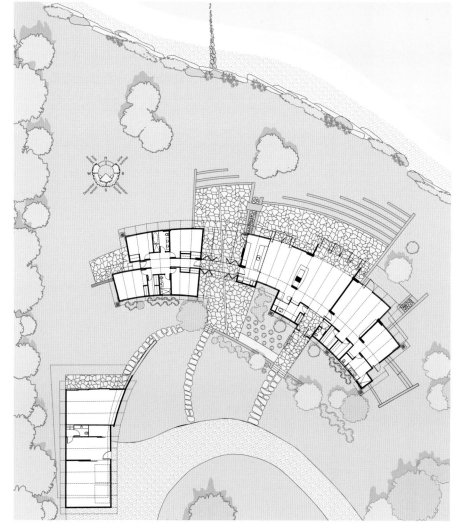

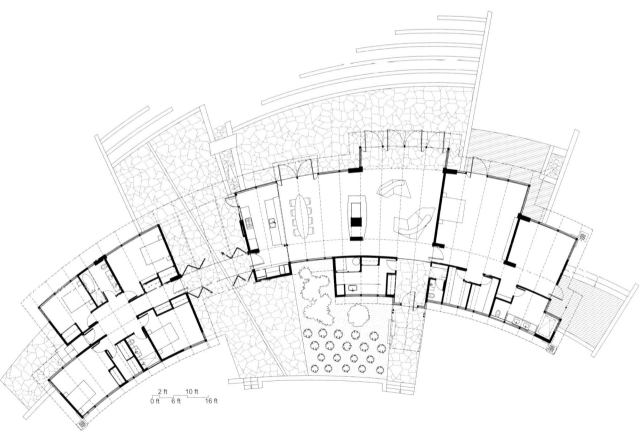

Opposite top: North elevation from beach
Opposite bottom left: Site plan
Opposite bottom right (top): South side looking east
Opposite bottom right (middle): Studio building
Opposite bottom right (bottom): Terrace with hallway doors opened
Top: South side view
Above: Floor plan

2 ft 10 ft
0 ft 6 ft 16 ft

Above: Terrace doors
Opposite top: Main entry
Opposite bottom: Corner detail

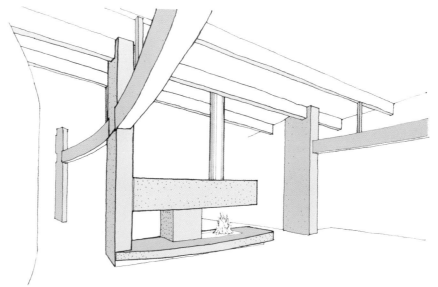

geometry and landscape element, mediating between buildings, gardens, forest and sea. The site was previously a trailer park set on a gravelled beach, requiring remediation to bring the seashore landscape back with indigenous vegetation. One of the owners is a painter and expressed interest in using colour as accent, providing contrast to a general palette of raw natural materials. Exterior walls of bright glass tile serve as punctuation points for the south courtyard. A lime-green tile accented with a bold orange stripe defines the west side of the courtyard. These lead on to a bright yellow glass tiled wall at the courtyard's center.

The interior is sparsely detailed with hardwood floors, architectural concrete, bluestone detailing and simple wall planes. Sculptural timber roofs float above walls of glass and cedar. A freestanding concrete fireplace between living and dining spaces furthers this design's clear and simple structural vocabulary. House and studio are heated with geothermal energy. All horizontal roofs are landscaped (green roofs), and the curving roof is clad in zinc. The structural frame is simply expressed through a post-and-beam system in Douglas fir. The door and window systems are integral within the timber frame structure. Understated details, a high standard to building craft and a dynamic dialogue with beach landscapes are the key themes here.

Opposite top: Dining room
Opposite bottom left: Master bedroom
Opposite bottom right: Master bathroom
Top: Primary structural elements sketch
Above: Kitchen

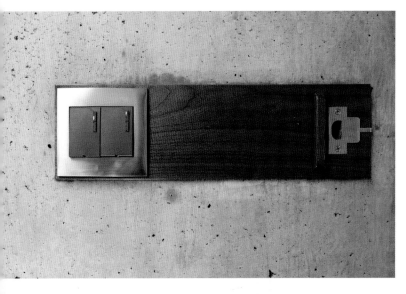

Previous pages: Great room
Top: Light switch and door-strike detail
Middle left: Structural detail
Middle right: Studio skylight
Above: Concrete column and timber connection
Opposite: Great room

FISHBONES HOUSE

STRUCTURE

Galiano Island, British Columbia
279 sq. m. (3000 sq. ft)
1993–1995

Like its wave-smoothed, water-moulded locale on a time-shaped sandstone shore, the design of the Fishbones House has been formed by the flow of water, weather and light. This design is also an important milestone in Blue Sky's evolution, as many of its ideas and principles shape subsequent work. The inspiration for these innovations starts with the sensuality of this sandstone shore, and the fluidity of the ocean channel it defines. The site is a long thin strip of land on the northwest coast of Galiano Island, in British Columbia's Southern Gulf Islands. The southwest side of the site is bounded by the roundly layered sandstone shelves and the fast-moving tidal rapids of Trincomali Channel. The northeast side rises sharply up a heavily forested bank to capture eastern light, providing a link to the road. At the north end of the site, a small point of arbutus and sandstone juts into the channel.

With a buildable footprint on the site extremely restricted, the layout of this house is necessarily linear, following the coastline. When approached from the up-hill side, flat roofs over the entrance, garage and service areas form grass terraces that emerge from the forest. On the sea side, the wave-like forms of a copper-clad roof roll along the ocean edge. Expressing the romantic and dynamic spirit of the site, the west wall curves along the shoreline and flows above the sculpted sandstone, anchoring a century-old cluster of Garry oaks. The spine of Fishbones House – a rational structural frame of a continuous 'backbone' ridge beam of 35cm-diameter (14 inches) cedar logs – parallels the shoreline and strings together the rooms below. Extending out from this spine are the bones – 23cm-diameter (9 inches) rounded roof rafters that set up an undulating rhythm along the shore, its ebbs and peaks echoing the action of the ocean. The ends of the log rafters extend boldly beyond the roofline, amplifying the wave effect and saluting the landscape. In detail and entirety, this house's structure recalls the skeleton of a large fish washed

Top: Site sandstone bluffs – form generator
Right: View along shore
Opposite top left: Roadside view
Opposite top right: Site plan

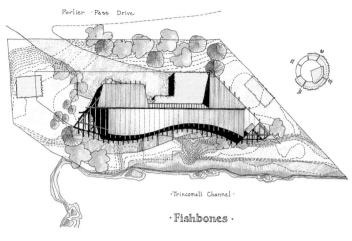

Porlier · Pass · Drive

·Trincomali Channel·

·Fishbones·

Below: West elevation
Bottom left: Roof structure – construction with architects
Bottom right: Exterior structure
Opposite top: Floor plan and south-west elevation
Opposite bottom left: Study model 'Fishbones'

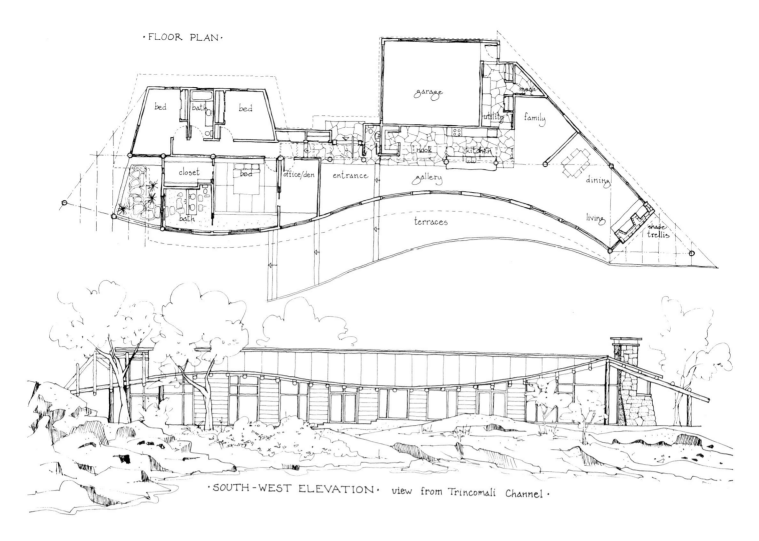

·FLOOR PLAN·

bed · bath · bed · garage · nook · utility · family · closet · bed · office/den · entrance · gallery · kitchen · dining · terraces · living · shade trellis

·SOUTH-WEST ELEVATION· view from Trincomali Channel·

up on shore and bleached in the sun. With their distortions and negotiations of form with gravity and site forces, these shapes also recall the waves that might have carried a fish here.

Different modulations of natural light and views define each space in the Fishbones House. On the western ocean-front side, the house opens to fine views of the Trincomali Channel and diamantine washes of light bounce off the waves. Along this edge, extended overhangs, trellises, screens and retained trees provide shade. Balancing the bold western light, coolly dappled forest light from the north and east filters through a continuous skylight that flanks the structural spine. With a main structure of post and beam set with log rafters contrasting with a secondary infill structure of conventional wood frame construction, the organic big picture is reconciled with everyday domestic details. In each room, a gentle rhythm and directionality results from roof rafters seeming to lift up and down. They rest on curving exterior walls that add lateral structural stability. Interior finishes of cherry wood and red cedar infuse warmth and a tactile quality to the whole building.

This home has been seminal for Blue Sky's evolving architectural vocabulary. The design steps away from the formal constraints of regular rectangular or even radial plan geometries to a more organic approach – all inspired by the natural flow of site. Using nature as a basis for design, the building is akin to an organism and mirrors the beauty and complexity of nature.

Opposite: Interior gallery
Top: View of kitchen from living room
Left: View of kitchen
Above: Post and beam – light detail

DUNLOP POINT HOUSE

STRUCTURE

Hornby Island, British Columbia
530 sq. m. (5700 sq. ft)
1976–1984

This early house was one of the first design/build projects designed by Blue Sky Architecture's predecessor firm Blue Sky Design, and the first design collaboration between Bo Helliwell and Michael McNamara. The house combines influences from Arthur Erickson, where Bo and Michael had worked, the back-to-the-land hand-built hippie designs of Hornby Island and an organic version of typical Arts and Crafts homes by California's Greene and Greene.

The house is organised around two intersecting axes, the first being an existing earth mound having hints of ancient native origins. The other axis, perpendicular to the first is the south-east view down Georgia Strait coincident with the alignments of the sunrise and sunset at the solstice. The house intentionally withdraws behind an ancient Indian mound, leaving a broad lawn and highly individualistic arbutus and fir trees as an extension of the seascape, helping shelter the house from the extreme southeasterly storms that buffet Dunlop Point. This siting also has the effect of reducing the perceived volume of the large house, guesthouse and swimming pool pavilions. Roof angles were derived from mimicking the surrounding windblown shrubbery.

A rationally linear plan, derived from Helliwell and McNamara's joint exposure to such Erickson designs as the Smith II and Graham houses, was embellished with found natural objects and a more organic range of details devised by Blue Sky, who also built it. A double grid was used in the planning, allowing for two-storey punctuations between the structural bays, providing a backfall of natural light into the main domestic spaces to complement and balance the bright seashore panorama. The structure is heavy hand-fitted log and timber post and beams with all structural joinery exposed. Wall and window planes are treated as curtain walls, making their location independent of the structural frame. Once framed in, the building was turned into a workshop, with millwork for doors and windows built by hand on the site using clear cedar. These highly finished elements contrast with the rough, heavy structure.

The Dunlop Point House was an advanced design and construction laboratory, the product of its sensitively unorthodox siting, internally expressed structure, and organically integrated details and re-use of local material. It established a set of principles and construction details that carried on into many subsequent projects. Inside and out, there is a focus on the craft of building – a harbinger of Blue Sky Architecture's key design principles.

Right: **Aerial view of Dunlop Point**
Opposite top: **Dunlop Point**
Opposite middle left: **Living room**
Opposite middle right: **Isometric sketch of main pavilion**
Opposite bottom left: **Post and beam/light detail**
Opposite bottom right: **Sketch of double grid structural elements**

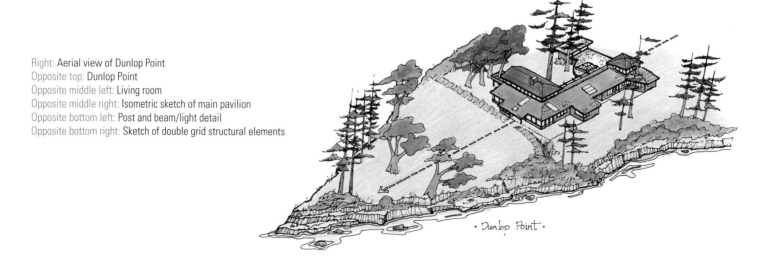

· Dunlop Point ·

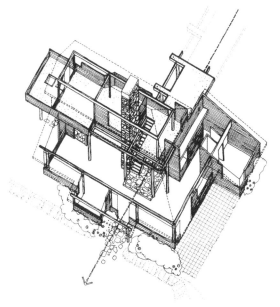

OAK GROVE HOUSE

TECTONIC

Salt Spring Island, British Columbia
233 sq. m. (2500 sq. ft)
2001–2011

Oak Grove House was originally designed as a retreat for living, sitting serenely in a beautiful oak meadow facing south, 290 metres (950 feet) above the Gulf Islands. Design team and builders took great care to preserve the natural landscape throughout the original construction and the building of an extension a decade later. Tracking along a flat contoured shelf on the hillside, the house has a radial plan, designed to pick up the curve established there by a Garry oak grove. A tilted and undulating roof opens up to ocean views and sunlight from the south.

The house's plan turns, a curving trail set across the hillside, moving dynamically from social rooms to private ones. Spaces are revealed in sequential glimpses as the hallway wraps around the hill. Trees and mossy rocks are dramatically close to a circular hallway, blending the residence into the hillside. The roof structure is exposed, revealing solid Douglas fir rafters and fir decking touching down on fir posts, which are in turn balanced on horizontal beams then vertical columns. Rafters rise and fall to create a gentle undulating roof blanketing all major spaces. A den, meditation room and gallery/hallway are set under the lower landscaped (green) roof. A split point in section between the two roofs allows for clerestory windows above the great room, balancing natural light and providing outlets for cross ventilation. Extended roof overhangs shelter the house from rain and sun.

Great attention has been paid to the finer grain of detail and builderly craftsmanship. Small scale and natural textures designed into the walls of this home encourage tactile contact, with a readily accessible palette of wood and stone. As is often the case for Blue Sky houses, the window system is integral with the timber frame structure. An assertive structural frame – including columns of round logs – imparts visual strength and warmth inside. Siding and doors include such fine details as cedar paneling inset with copper inlay. Finessed with these appointments, the house's beauty rises in response to its glorious setting.

Top: Concept sketch
Right: House from south
Opposite top left and right: Outdoor room

Below: Floor plan
Bottom: House following curve of hillside
Opposite top left: Roof detail
Opposite top right: Section
Opposite middle: Entry pavilion
Opposite bottom: House from east

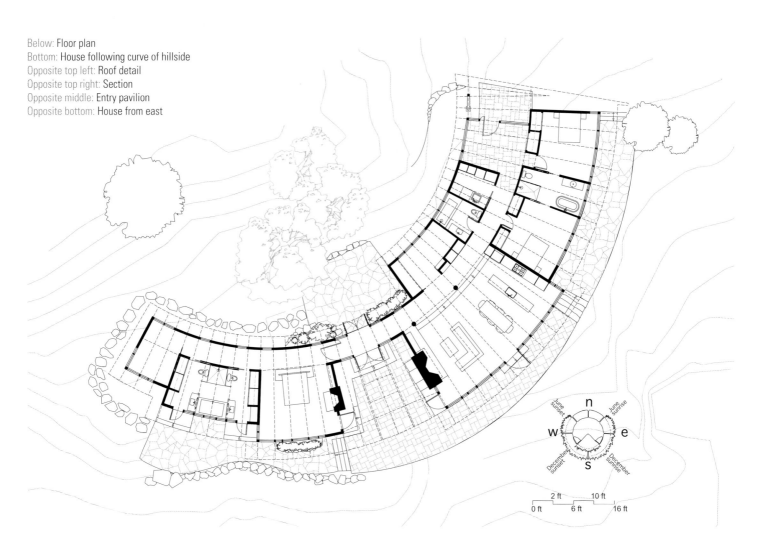

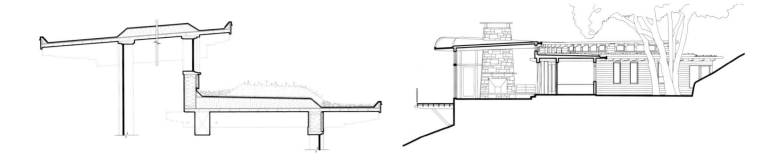

A covered outdoor room means alfresco dining and socialising is possible all through the year, while also serving to split the floorplan between areas for social activities and bedrooms. The entrance, guest area, office area, great room and kitchen are linked to the main bedroom suite by a transparent hallway that is shaped around the oak grove and the outdoor room.

Eight years after completion, subsequent owners of the house had Blue Sky design additional spaces for the home: a new bedroom, bathroom and a gallery entrance. The home continues as a family retreat but has also become a gallery for an art collection. The redesigned entrance area was enlarged to house a dynamic large canvas complemented by a corner window that frames the hillside and trees. One of Blue Sky's most ravishing entrance experiences, this room announces all of the house's intention with verve and vigour.

Previous pages: Great room view
Opposite top left: Entrance
Opposite top right: Main hall/gallery
Opposite bottom: Great room from kitchen
Top: Interior of entrance pavilion
Left: Entry to master suite
Above: Master ensuite bath

Top: Night view from southeast
Above: Inside entry pavilion
Opposite: Great room

RAINFOREST HOUSE

TECTONIC

Tofino, British Columbia
232 sq. m. (2500 sq. ft)
2006–2008

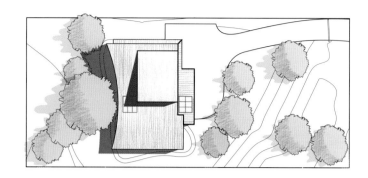

The inspiration for this house is the old-growth rainforest on the west coast of Vancouver Island, which has an ancient majesty that surrounds and overwhelms. Clad in western red cedar inside and out, the house is set in a grove of giant western red cedars, and its simple shed roof rises up to salute the towering trees.

The strength and beauty of the flanking wild forest has architectural expression in the use of a structural timber frame. The house is clad in western red cedar shingles and clear cedar siding. The cedar shingles blend with the natural environment and are a durable skin for the cool wet climate of the Pacific Northwest. The glass-roofed outdoor room on the north side of the house brings light into the house and provides a sheltered place to sit in the forest during the frequent grey days, with their extended light drizzle or rain. Partially clad in clear horizontal red cedar, this same cedar siding is used on the tall interior feature wall at the entry, which connects and dissolves separations of interior and exterior space. A large and finely crafted red cedar mask carved by a West Coast First Nations artist is the visual focus of this wall.

Pre-fabricated off-site, an exposed Douglas fir timber frame adds visual strength and interlaces horizontal and vertical, enforcing the dedication to craft in the house. A verandah wraps around the south or road-oriented side of the house, providing another sheltered outdoor area, and breaking down the scale of the high south wall.

The house features a range of rooms to meet the needs of visits from an extended family of three generations. Located next to a popular surfing beach, there is an outdoor surf room with an outdoor shower and surfboard lockers. The house is designed as a natural extension of both ocean and forest, in its forms and in its appointments. The selection and detailing of coastal timber frame and wooden finishes makes for a site-specific essay in the transformation of forest into culture – a contemporary inhabitable analogue to the cedar mask.

Top: Site plan
Above: East façade
Above right: Forest view from northwest
Opposite top: Floor plan
Opposite bottom: South side

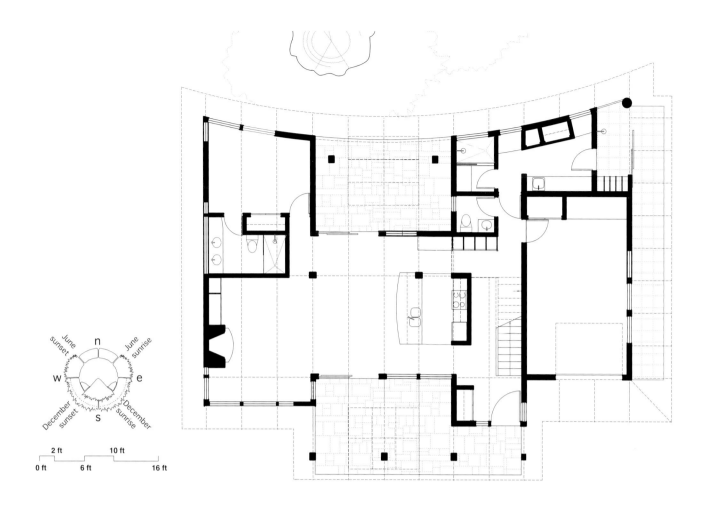

Previous pages: North façade and outdoor room
Below left: Stair detail
Below middle: View from upper landing
Right: Kitchen and structure
Below: Living room
Opposite: Dining room

BRIDGE HOUSE

TECTONIC

Denman Island, British Columbia
205 sq. m. (2200 sq. ft)
1991–1996

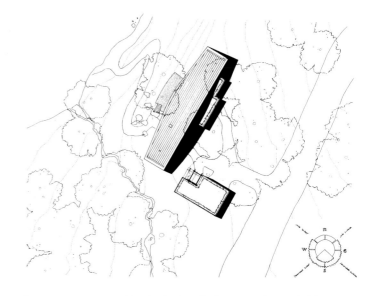

Denman Island is flatter, tamer and more agricultural than adjacent Hornby Island, locale of Blue Sky Architecture's first constructions. The clients bought the site of this house, a slightly sloped section of seashore overlooking Baynes Sound on the west side of the island. The German-born lady of the house had a taste for European modernism, while the man was a dedicated environmentalist. They wanted a modest retirement home that could accommodate family visits, accentuate their established love of coastal aesthetics, and serve as backdrop to their collection of fine antique furniture.

When the architects first surveyed the site, they noticed a trail carved through the forest by Denman residents and animals in order to gain access to the sand and gravel beach on the other side. This existing

pathway was preserved by designing the house to form a bridge over it. The resulting plan is long and linear, with all major rooms stretched parallel to the ocean in order to maximise views and light. The bridge design metaphor was implemented in two senses: first, with the house literally bridging over the pre-existing path from forest to ocean; and second, with a trestle structure that shapes and supports the long curving roof that arches through the house.

On the ocean side, an arched roof volume bows outward. At the peak of this bow, a concave space is carved out of the façade, with an extended cantilevered roof sheltering it. A bridge room connects principal social spaces with a self-contained, two-bedroom guesthouse that accommodates children and grandchildren. To ensure acoustic

Opposite top: Site plan
Opposite bottom: Roadside elevation from northeast
Left: Ocean terrace
Below: Beachside elevation

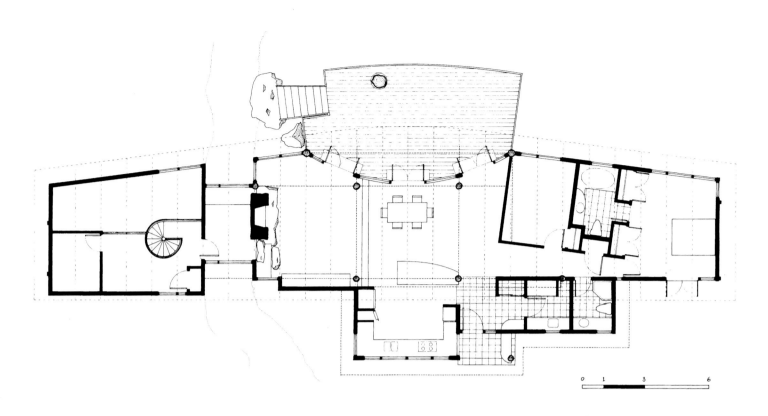

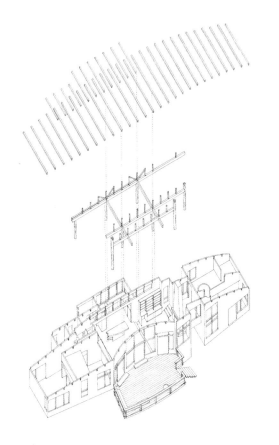

privacy, at the house's opposite end is the owner's bedroom suite and home office. The arched roof structure is economically formed with a light raftered ceiling. Supporting each rafter, a grid of posts, four by four, bear on horizontal beams. This eliminates the need for pre-manufactured curving laminated beams, and recalls timber trestle railway bridges, another sense of Blue Sky's driving metaphor. Although the architects had used this post-and-beam and raftered structure in previous designs, this was the purest and simplest expression yet of this idea, and these same features are used in later designs.

Much of the house's framing was milled from trees cleared from the building site. House alignment was conceived to retain as many mature trees as possible. Both the sandstone surrounding the fireplace, and the western maple floorboards are supplied from Denman Island. Local materials integrate the building physically and spiritually into its site. Bridge House is remarkable for the clarity of its concept, floor plan, section and structure, all organised around a bridge metaphor that does not compromise habitation, but informs a framework for its daily disposition.

Opposite top: Main floor plan
Opposite bottom: Dining room to living room
Top: Exploded axonometric
Left: Great room
Above: Stair detail

BENCH SPIRAL HOUSE

TECTONIC

Hornby Island, British Columbia
353 sq. m. (3800 sq. ft)
1981–1983/1996

· south elevation ·

During their first visit to Hornby Island in 1980, the Cleveland-based clients hiked up Mount Geoffrey to the Bench, a wide ledge perched 152 metres (500 feet) above sea level. There are spectacular views from here west to Vancouver Island's mountains and Strathcona Park, and north along the open waters of Georgia Strait. After picnicking here and being enchanted by the landscape, they discovered a "For Sale" sign. After purchasing the land, they hired Blue Sky Design to design and build what would become their retirement home.

In 1981, Blue Sky Design was working as a new designer-build firm, so construction drawings were not formal documents set in stone, or even on paper! Instead, they set the stage for a building process with creative flexibility, allowing for design development that could adapt to building materials, spaces, light, views and natural artifacts as they became apparent or available. To commence this design project, builder Tim Wyndham and designer Bo Helliwell did a detailed survey of the topography, including locating all major trees. With this unusually detailed site information, the spiral design was conceived and developed by Helliwell with a small model crafted to guide actual construction – there were few drawings. For the Bench Spiral House, the building was constructed intuitively.

The house sits on the crest of a small hill surrounded by arbutus trees. After carefully preparing the site, steel pins were set at the focus points of the spiral, and then its increasing radials marked out sequentially with string. These served as reference points to generate the curves of its plan and to centre the golden-mean proportions of its overall plan. The spiral's two focal points are the earthbound stone mass of the fireplace anchored into the hillside; and the skyward-bound curving staircase ascending to the lookout tower – the constructional and occupational hearts of the house. Gravity and lift, and heavy mass and light play off each other as plan conception turned into markings, then floors and walls.

Eschewing consistency for the possibilities of the site, this house is a dance between conventional wood framing and exposed post-and-beam construction. Indigenous woods are used: Douglas fir, red cedar and yellow cedar. Fine millwork is finished in American cherry. Local granite and sandstone are used in the masonry fireplace and for the house's skirted base. One of BC's first architect-designed landscaped or 'green' roof was a key element in visually marrying house to hilltop. Respecting the daily rituals of clients who had become friends, a progression of inhabitation steps down the hillside through the house as each day passes. Breakfasts and morning chats usually take place in the corner adjacent to the kitchen. Summer afternoons are spent on the uphill, sheltered terrace and flower garden, with sunset evenings in the dining room. As the day finishes, the owners use their mountainside perch to moon-gaze, then nestle into chairs in front of the monumental fireplace.

In ensuing years the house has continued to grow organically with the client's extended family; first a studio was built, then the guest area expanded, and finally an autonomous additional guest suite was added. In order not to affect the existing house and its spiral-generated views, each addition extended to the north. Like parent with child then grandchild, the house's elaborations further integrated into the landscape while taking advantage of site opportunities of topography, views and light.

The design and construction of the Bench Spiral House was an exciting test case for expanding spatial understanding, architecture as sculpture and the craft of timber framing and fine millwork finishing. This home results from the intersection of influences on Helliwell's architectural career; John Ruskin's ideas of pride of workmanship; Greene and Greene's Arts and Crafts workmanship; Vincent Scully's take on the American Shingle Style; and former employer Etienne Gaboury's passion for continuous light and space. But as important as any of these, were the rough-hewn hand-built Hornby hippy experiments of the 1970s and others.

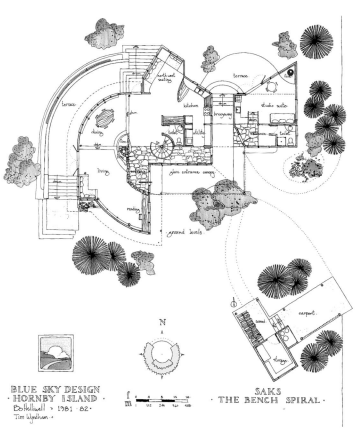

BLUE SKY DESIGN
· HORNBY ISLAND
Bo Helliwell · 1981 · 82
Tim Wyndham ·

SAKS
· THE BENCH SPIRAL ·

SOLAR CREST HOUSE

SYSTEMS

Sidney Island, British Columbia
260 sq. m. (2800 sq. ft)
2005–2010

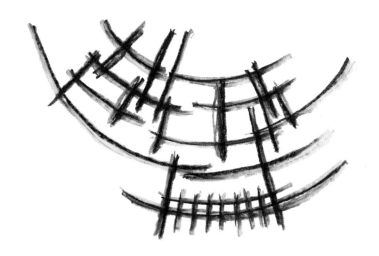

Embracing a rugged rocky ridge on a remote island in Juan de Fuca Strait, Solar Crest House is a completely off-grid home and garden. In section and plan, it combines a studied geometric formality with organic and sensuous elements that merge with its surrounding landscape of rounded glaciated granite. The plan of the house is an arc following the sun and the hill's crest opening to southern light and views across the Strait to the Olympic Mountains in Washington State. In section, the roof undulates – a living sculpture responding to the hierarchy of spatial use, the opportunities of sun, air, views and the shape of the land itself. On the entrance garden side, lower flat roofs maximise light penetration into the house's centre and assist natural ventilation throughout.

The building is off all energy grids and is oriented to maximise solar gain. Its central spaces are transparent so that the southern sun penetrates deeply into interior spaces, warming floors and walls. Ocean views to the south and west are open to all spaces, including the south-facing outdoor room and terraces. The only level outdoor spaces on the site are the terraces that had to be constructed from scratch. These cover five cisterns holding 141,000 litres (37,000 gallons) of rainwater collected from roof surfaces, for use in all domestic and landscape purposes and available for fire-fighting. To power the home, 26 solar photovoltaic panels are located out of sight from inside the house, leaning against the terrace's curving south wall. When the electrical battery storage is low, a back-up diesel generator takes over. Other sustainable features are a wind turbine, on-demand hot water, radiant in-floor heating, LED lighting, energy-efficient appliances, low-flush toilets and on-site vegetable gardens.

Because of a large introduced deer population on the island, all gardens need high fencing as protection. The fencing is designed to be either visually non-obtrusive or a contrasting horizontal cedar

Top: Concept sketch
Right: View from south
Opposite top: Site plan

116

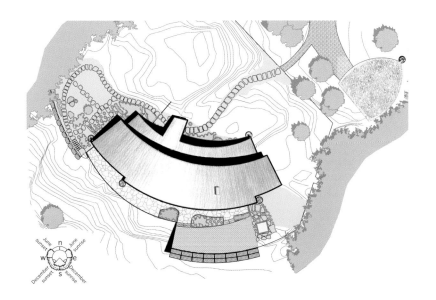

screen landscape feature. The remote island has only private boat access and no local services, so all construction materials had to be moved by small barge with all attendant difficulties of weather, tides, and off-loading onto a small ramp. As with most Blue Sky buildings, wood frame was the construction choice, being a relatively lightweight, easily movable and easy-to-use material. Most of the fir and cedar used in the house is local, harvested and milled on nearby Vancouver Island. Large glass walls lining the dining room and adjacent entrance hall fully slide back to open the home to terrace, views and outdoor living. The inclusion of alternative energy systems enables the home to be situated in a stunningly beautiful, remote landscape completely free of organised energy grids and dependent only on the natural cycles surrounding it.

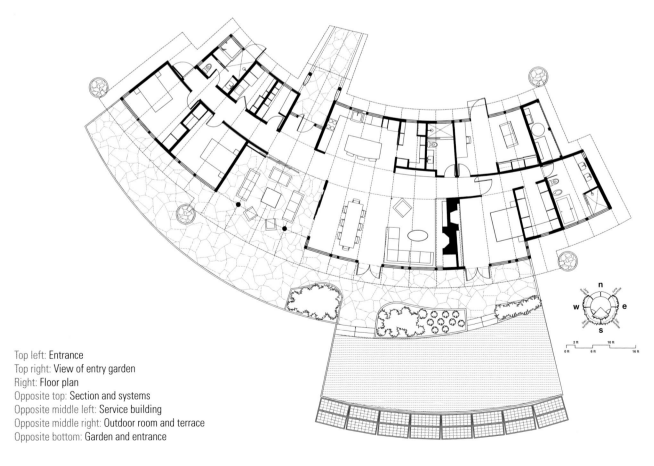

Top left: Entrance
Top right: View of entry garden
Right: Floor plan
Opposite top: Section and systems
Opposite middle left: Service building
Opposite middle right: Outdoor room and terrace
Opposite bottom: Garden and entrance

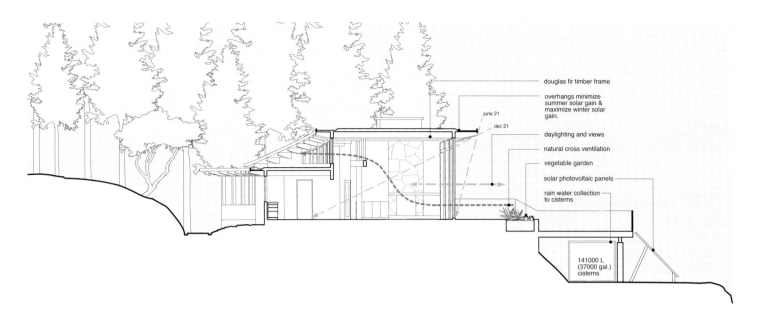

douglas fir timber frame

overhangs minimize
summer solar gain &
maximize winter solar
gain.

june 21

dec 21

daylighting and views

natural cross ventilation

vegetable garden

solar photovoltaic panels

rain water collection
to cisterns

141000 L
(37000 gal.)
cisterns

Opposite top: Living/dining
Opposite bottom: South elevation with solar panels
Top left: Living/dining
Top right: Outdoor room
Above: Kitchen

GULLWING HOUSE

SYSTEMS

Hornby Island, British Columbia
205 sq. m. (2200 sq. ft)
1983–1985

This is an early Blue Sky Design House, designed by Bo Helliwell and Michael McNamara. The sculptural lines of the roof and a range of structural/elevational details guide many later houses by this firm, and its successor, Helliwell + Smith • Blue Sky Architecture. The owners purchased this meadow-like site at the end of the best sand beach on Hornby Island, and approached Blue Sky Design with a number of strong ideas. The couple had backgrounds in urban planning and had taken part in environmental and social planning for the Gulf Islands. In addition, they brought to the design a small collection of salvaged building elements such as recycled flooring and a door from a tugboat, which were incorporated into their

new house. The tugboat door was twinned to provide access and porthole windows to an upper balcony, while the recycled flooring now graces the living/dining room.

The flanking pair of low roofs shape architectural/ornithological 'wings,' thereby generating the "gullwing" name for this shore-nesting domicile. A double-storey atrium in the house's centre divides the social spaces from bedrooms and provides a passive solar heat sink. On the south-facing roof wing, solar hot water panels provide hot water for the home – again, an early application of now much more accepted green building technologies. Interior

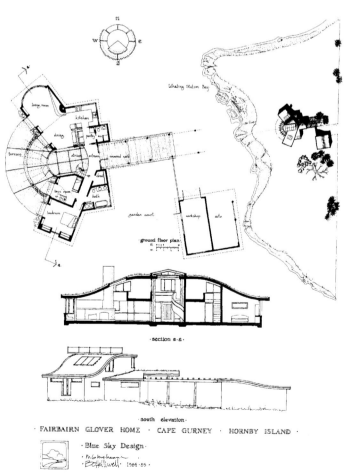

· FAIRBAIRN GLOVER HOME · CAPE GURNEY · HORNBY ISLAND ·

· Blue Sky Design ·

spaces were designed to be curving, calm and embracing. Inside, a soft palette of white walls contrasts with the natural colours of wood and stone. Over time, the landscape roof has blended with the adjoining meadow flowers and a trellis that supports a thriving grapevine that has become a green wall.

This home was an early example of using both active and passive solar energy as well as green roofs. A graceful and symmetrical roof rises up from the meadow, and because it is planted with meadow grass and flowers, there is a blurring between setting and building.

Opposite left: Terrace
Opposite right: Site plan, plan, elevation, section
Top: Living room
Left: Atrium
Above: West elevation

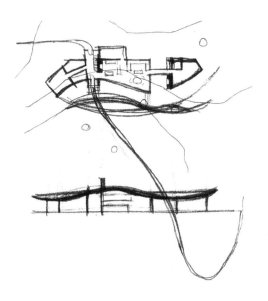

DEER PATH HOUSE

SYSTEMS

Gambier Island, British Columbia
186 sq. m. (2000 sq. ft)
2000–2003

Responding to the sweeping movement of the land and the shoreline's undulations, the Deer Path House has a tectonic topography arising from the form and structure of its roof. The lineal floor plan is laid out to echo a path through the woods used by deer. Living spaces are open to sun and water views to the south, while the service spaces aligned on the north are more enclosed. The north elevation is orthogonal and its forest-side window openings respond to site opportunities in their size and location. The south elevation is a three-dimensional curve, reflecting site contours and line of the shore. With the exception of structurally necessary shear panels, this side is entirely glazed. Extended roof overhangs, flanking evergreen forest and a design for natural ventilation all combine to keep the house pleasantly temperate year round. A 3-metre-high cube crate made of stainless steel wire containing coiled PVC pipe filled with inert liquid is submerged in the ocean. This heat sink functions as a water source geo-exchange system to provide heating.

The airily sculptural roof-forms are brought back to earth by two monumental granite chimney stacks, visual and physical anchors. The house opens generously towards the water on its south side, spreading natural light throughout its slender, shore-seeking layout. Vertical structural framing and window divisions extend the rhythm of the adjacent forest to the interior, filtering light and view. This heavily forested building site focuses on a small cove and an exposed granite peninsula to the south. While Gambier Island is not far from Horseshoe Bay's ferry terminal, there is no direct vehicular ferry access to the island. Accordingly, no heavy machinery was used for site preparation. This encouraged shaping a plan that is continuous following existing grades and vegetation.

This house builds on West Coast modernist traditions by having interior living environments extend seamlessly into adjacent landscapes. While interior spaces are complex, house structure is cleanly expressed,

Top: Concept sketch
Above left: View of house and terrace
Above right: Site plan
Opposite top: View from west
Opposite bottom: View from east

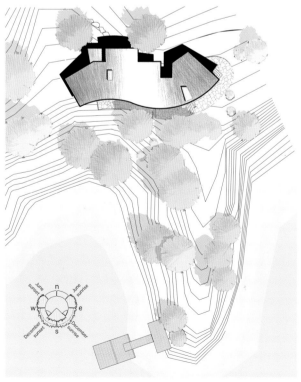

Below: Section and systems
Bottom left (top): Water view from loft
Bottom left (bottom): Outdoor room
Bottom right: Living room
Opposite top: Floor plan
Opposite bottom: Front door view to water

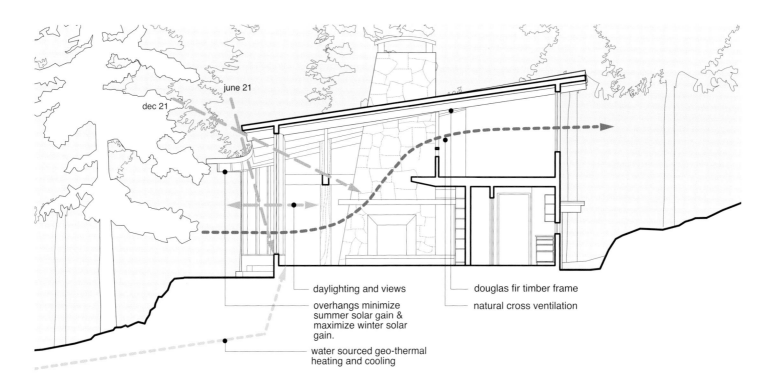

june 21

dec 21

daylighting and views

overhangs minimize summer solar gain & maximize winter solar gain.

water sourced geo-thermal heating and cooling

douglas fir timber frame

natural cross ventilation

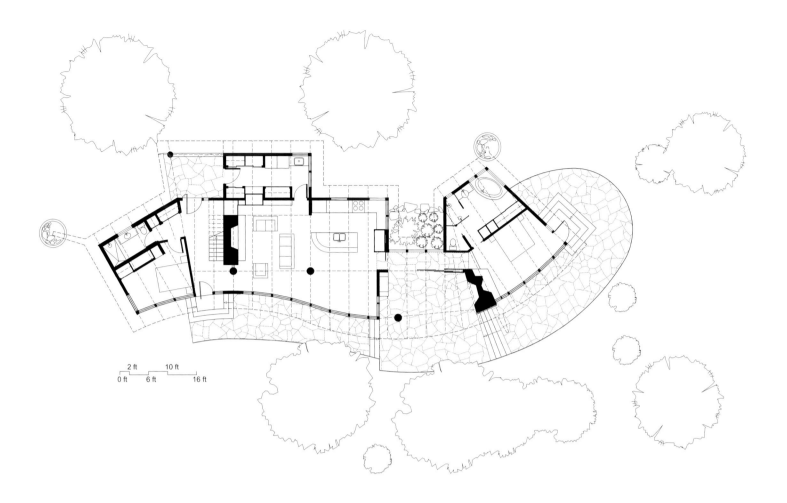

using a palette of natural materials assembled out of a commitment to simplicity and economy. Key structural columns are Douglas fir logs obtained from clearing the house's building site. The exact height for the bearing points of each timber rafter was calculated and each of these supported on vertical posts with a cross section of 10cm by 10 cm (four inches by four inches), which themselves sit on horizontal beams or window mullions. The bent roof decking acts as a shell structure, strengthening and tying together the construction. The roof billows and flexes through the landscape, rising and falling in accordance with functional needs in the spaces below. When walking on the roof, you feel you are on a living organism.

The house exhibits two major spatial conditions, which define the sleeping areas as separate from the central living, eating and kitchen zone. At the east end, the main bedroom suite is linked to these social areas through a glass hallway. This hallway flanks a covered outdoor room with granite fireplace. The hall's south side consists of glass panels sliding into pocket slots, opening interiors to this 'outdoor room' and sublime views towards the point. The hall's north side forms one edge of a small moss and fern garden. At the west end of the house, the guest bedroom is separated from the living room by the entrance and stair hall. These layout decisions combine to create movement through the house, connecting forest trails and the access road to the north with a path down to the dock area, its maritime 'front door'.

ASSINIBOINE RIVER HOUSE

Winnipeg, Manitoba
236 sq. m. (2540 sq. ft)
2004–2007

Most, but not all of Blue Sky's domestic designs are for remote coastal sites. Neither remote nor coastal, this is an urban house for Winnipeg's historic but gentrifying inner city neighbourhood of Wolseley. It presents a very different set of design challenges. Unlike the spatial freedoms afforded most Blue Sky projects for wilder and more remote sites, the potential built space or 'building envelope' here was determined by the City of Winnipeg's lot setback and zoning regulations. With its urban location, and proximity to neighbouring houses, the home had specific requirements for privacy.

In addition, centre-of-continent Winnipeg's climate is dramatically different than that of coastal British Columbia, with extremes ranging from a dry minus-40 degrees (the same in both Celsius and Fahrenheit) in winter to a humid summer where temperatures can rise to the high 30s in degrees Celsius. Winter dryness provides a challenge to exterior material choices, resulting in a mix of native limestone and stucco with limited cedar wood accents.

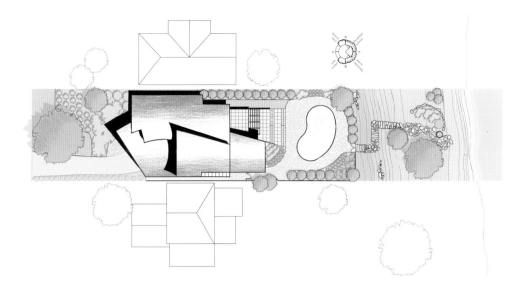

Opposite top left: Stair detail
Opposite bottom left: South elevation
Below: Street view
Left: Site plan

This home was designed for a family of four. The entrance and garage are set at an angle from the street. They are connected to a long hall that curves through the house and this alignment inflects the adjacent rooms. The stairwell doubles as a lightwell, connecting the three floors and pulling prairie light from a clerestory window deep down into interior spaces. In an interior detail inspired by such Alvar Aalto domestic designs as the Villa Mairea, the stairwell is flanked by vertical screens of hardwood dowels of varying diameter. This detail also references small broadleaf prairie forests and is used to diffuse light while creating semi-transparent room-to-room transitions. The intense light of the prairie skies is filtered through these screens, mimicking the dappled light of local aspen forests. A screened porch on the south side of the home opens to a garden area with a swimming pool and terrace stepping down to the banks of the slow-moving Assiniboine River.

The lesson of Assiniboine House is that there is no fundamental difference in designing urban as opposed to rural houses. Design principles developed by Blue Sky for wilder landscapes all apply, whether responding to site contingencies; dealing with light regimes and exploiting them spatially; developing an appropriate palette of materials; or perhaps most of all, shaping spaces that flow and interact with the needs of everyday life.

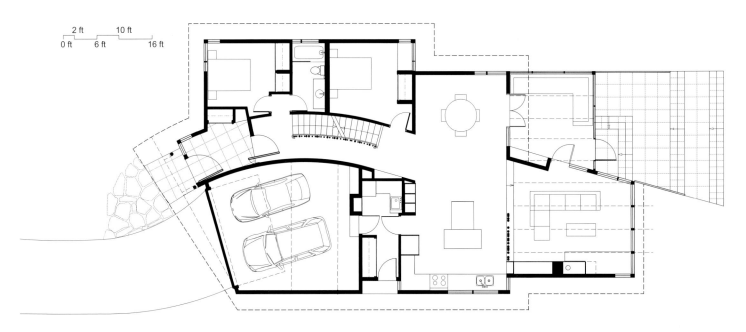

Opposite top: Floor plan
Opposite bottom left: Screened porch
Opposite bottom right: Living room
Top: Living room to hallway
Left: Stair
Above: Timber and stone detail

Above: Living/Kitchen

CHESTERMAN BEACH HOMES

Tofino, British Columbia
39 Townhouses covering a total
floor area of 3985 sq. m. (42,900 sq. ft)
1996–2000

The curved rooflines of these waterfront pavilions containing three, four and five-townhouse buildings evoke the form of rolling ocean waves. Smaller curved roof dormers – similarly curved – recall flocks of small shorebirds soaring above Tofino's sandy beaches. These 39 homes are located on a 1.7-hectare (4.3 acres) site facing west onto some of the wildest and most beautiful beaches on the west coast of Vancouver Island. The disposition of the townhouse buildings onto the site allows for ocean views from each beach residence, with a communal green and play areas set at their centre. The Chesterman Beach site was logged 20 years ago, and is just a few miles north of Pacific Rim National Park Reserve. To help restore the former forest landscape, species of solely native flora are planted.

Most parking areas are partly recessed into the gently sloping site and have landscaped roofs. These green roofs extend the sense of the communal garden areas to inland as well as ocean-view sides of the housing. A small wetlands area on site was retained to permit site drainage and to provide additional natural habitat. The narrow beachfront property to the west has been left as a green space reserve, including a public path to Chesterman Beach.

The rhythm of each housing block's massing was designed so that individually and collectively they read as a cohesive whole. The western row of homes curve down to maximise afternoon light penetration, while the eastern row rises up to grab morning light and

Opposite top: Sketch
Opposite bottom: Site plan
Left: Aerial view of site
Below: View from beach
Bottom: East view of units

views across the village green. The architectural design and overall site plan are conceived to maximise enjoyment of views towards the Pacific surf and spectacular sunsets. Each format of housing block is paired to shape a wave form, and to provide a micro- and macro-sense of visual harmony throughout the complex. All 39 units have on-grade entrances with private terraces, and view balconies. The homes range in size from 68 sq. m. (730 sq. ft) to 125 sq. m. (1350 sq. ft).

The whole effect makes for a funky coastal village feel, with architectural detailing and a custom colour palette evoking a rustic West Coast spirit. The flexibility of hybrid timber frames here has empowered a variety of sculptural buildings and spaces. Exterior walls are clad with heavily textured board-and-batten cedar siding. Entrance areas are finished in cedar shingles, with trims in natural cedar. The towers are painted in strong contrasting colours to accentuate these vertical elements.

Here, a precious seaside site has been purposely underdeveloped to maintain a greater presence of natural garden and forest. The community that has formed here is a mix of permanent residents of Tofino and those who use it periodically as seasonal housing. All have been brought together here by a sense of visual unity and community in a wildly beautiful seaside forest.

Top: View south towards forest
Above: View west with green carport roof
Opposite top: Triplex entry elevation
Opposite bottom: Interior

WAKEFIELD BEACH HOMES

COMMUNITY

Sechelt, British Columbia
40 Townhouses and Houses covering a total
floor area of 8274 sq. m. (89,065 sq. ft.)
2005–2009

This 2-hectare (5 acres) south-facing oceanfront site slopes down to a beautiful, pebble beach with views of Georgia Strait, the Trail Islands and Vancouver Island. Located on the western edge of the town of Sechelt, the development objectives here were to create a beach community based on sustainable design principles. Replacing the existing Wakefield Inn, this project required an extended public consultation and re-zoning process, which was much more complex than for Blue Sky's single-family projects. Wakefield's core design strategy was to engage each home with the ocean visually, and for each to have a generous outdoor living space. The opportunity was to create a sense of community through density, which in turn finances the developer's donation of a public park with easy public access to the seashore.

Notions of building a completely new community and enhancing environmental conditions were part of the project from the beginning, originating from a progressive developer having local roots. This site was the previous home of the Wakefield Resort, one of the oldest resort developments on British Columbia's Sunshine Coast. Run down after years of marginal operations and non-investment, its beloved pub and prime stretch of shoreline contained history and memories for the local community. An initial 'envisioning session' was held with the developer, architects, planning staff, mayor, parks board, local historian and interested community members to determine what the project should be. Initial planning strategies called for a dense beach community retaining memories of the past, but connected to the larger community, with a dedicated public park having beach access and easy connection to the local bus system. Initial environmental strategies included geo-thermal heating and cooling, green roofs, recycled timbers from the former Wakefield Inn, use of prefabricated wood panels and timber frames harvested from sustainable forests

Top: Roofscape
Right: Beachfront houses
Opposite top: Rendering

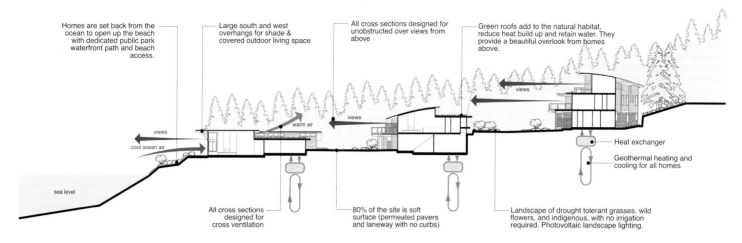

Homes are set back from the ocean to open up the beach with dedicated public park waterfront path and beach access.

Large south and west overhangs for shade & covered outdoor living space

All cross sections designed for unobstructed over views from above

Green roofs add to the natural habitat, reduce heat build up and retain water. They provide a beautiful overlook from homes above.

views

views

warm air

views

Heat exchanger

views

cool ocean air

Geothermal heating and cooling for all homes

sea level

All cross sections designed for cross ventilation

80% of the site is soft surface (permeated pavers and laneway with no curbs)

Landscape of drought tolerant grasses, wild flowers, and indigenous, with no irrigation required. Photovoltaic landscape lighting.

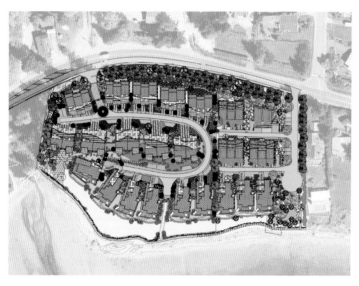

and supplied by local mills, high-performance window glazing, indigenous landscape planting, permeable surfaces for natural site drainage, solar landscape lighting, sediment and erosion control and waste management through sustainable construction practice.

Site planning concerns were to make optimal utilisation of the land, while amplifying its natural attributes. As for architecture, the design seeks forms, details and housing clusters appropriate to the region and local traditions. A sense of community that is so often lacking in new developments was quite literally 'built in' at Wakefield Beach Homes. On its west side there is a dedicated public park with a pedestrian path to the beach, while at the eastern edge there is public access and a beach featuring a small boat launch and waterfront path. There is easy access for pedestrians and biking paths on the site and an on-site bus shelter provided by the developer.

Blue Sky devised a range of housing types, from three-bedroom triplexes, two-bedroom duplexes, and three-bedroom single-family homes. There is a social mix from families to empty nesters to weekend users, thanks to the planned variety in housing types. Wakefield Beach Homes is a trailblazer in medium-density living in a region that tends to apply typical suburban models to its increasingly rare stretches of undeveloped waterfront. Blue Sky puts more new residents in close contact with the shore. The housing clusters have been arrayed ingeniously to maximise water views between and through the ranks of housing. After a thorough site study, the sectional arrangements of units were designed to ensure each home has an unrestricted ocean view from its main living space. Curving vaulted roofs highlight their timber structure and provide opportunities for north-facing clerestories. The clerestory balances direct and water-reflected south light from the seaside, creating sensuous and dynamic main living spaces and provides natural cross ventilation. With each row of residences marching up from the shore to the top of the property, these glinting curved roofs evoke breaking waves coming in off the Pacific.

Each home has geo-exchange heating and cooling systems, high-performance window glazing and natural local materials. The landscape roofs help reduce heat build-up and retain water, reducing the typical flush of water to the storm water systems. Eighty percent of the site and buildings are soft-surfaced with permeable pavers, landscaping

Top: Site section
Middle left: Site plan
Middle right: Overall view
Opposite top: Indoor and outdoor spaces at beachfront unit
Opposite bottom: Covered beachside terrace

and curb-free laneways. Throughout the site, indigenous and drought-resistant plantings, including grasses, wild flowers, sedums, local trees and shrubs eliminate the need for irrigation, even in the driest summer months. The dedicated public park has been retained as a natural forest with a landscaped path to the beach. The seashore edge has been bermed and planted with indigenous sea grasses. A natural path with elevated boardwalk over sensitive wetland areas along the seashore gives the public easy access to the beach.

When the project was initially marketed, the most significant concerns buyers had were about the geothermal energy and the green roofs. It was the first market project in the area to incorporate these elements. After a short while, these became the most popular selling features, and the project has served to educate the public about green strategies for living. Similarly, this housing absorbs solar energy in the winter months thanks to south-facing windows, while large overhangs protect from solar gain in the summer. The same is true for natural ventilation via convection currents, courtesy of low windows along the south side and high clerestory windows on the north.

In a region scarred by tacky strip malls and bland low-density subdivisions, Wakefield Homes established a benchmark for contemporary building and living on the Sunshine Coast. The density and community that it creates and the public amenities with park and beach access it provides give back to the larger coastal community.

BO HELLIWELL

Born in 1944, Bo Helliwell grew up in the northwestern Ontario city of Thunder Bay. The city represents all key Canadian landscapes: the hardwood forests and Canadian Shield to the east; crisp light and bright skies to the west; and the wilderness of forest and bog to the north. Thunder Bay is a grain port on Lake Superior, its waterfront dominated by a stunning collection of cast concrete grain silos, a building form so beloved by Le Corbusier that he labeled them "the first fruits of the new era" of modernism, where an "engineer's aesthetic" would prevail over historicist sentimentality. The grain elevators were a favoured childhood destination for Bo's winter ice skating adventures, and summers were spent immersed in nature at the family cottage. His first direct contact with architecture came when he found an old set of blueprints, prompting a childhood fascination for their sense of a world in miniature and the graphic intensity of an intense blue ground filled with intricate white lines. By the age of 10, Bo Helliwell was announcing that he wanted to become an architect, despite never having met one.

That situation changed after his department store manager father was transferred to Winnipeg when Bo was 15 years old. One of his close high-school friends was the son of John Russell, Dean of Architecture at the University of Manitoba, and Helliwell spent much time in their house, surrounded by their collection of books and modernist art. Russell had built the Manitoba programme into Canada's most advanced citadel of modernism, establishing to a line of influential designers ranging from Sydney's Harry Seidler, to Toronto's John C. Parkin and Vancouver's John and Patricia Patkau.

Helliwell entered Manitoba's Bachelor of Architecture programme in 1963. The first-year studio studies were then dominated by Bauhaus-derived graphic exercises in formal composition. He spent the summer working in the faculty's slide library rather than better-paying construction sites because of the opportunities it provided to advance his knowledge of art and architectural history. During his first encounters with the design of buildings in his second year, Helliwell came under the influence of Gustavo da Roza, a Hong Kong native who was then designing a string of bold houses and beginning work on the Winnipeg Art Gallery, buildings much admired both locally and nationally. Helliwell's experience with so tough and charismatic teacher as Da Roza showed him that there was still much to learn about architecture, both inside and outside the academy.

He took a year out to work for Manitoba graduate Etienne Gaboury, then continued working in the firm during summer vacations, right through to graduation.

Gaboury's buildings have a wider palette of forms and symbols than the minimalist Da Roza, and he has interest in the philosophical and cultural frameworks for design. Gaboury derived a theory of windows adapted to the prairie landscape in a civic centre design for the francophone suburb of St. Boniface, and Helliwell worked on the architect's own riverside house for his large family, a design strikingly predictive of his own work on Hornby Island fifteen years later. The best-known of the Gaboury designs that Helliwell worked on was the Eglise du Précieux-Sang in Winnipeg. Audacious spatially, materially and structurally, the church was a highlight of bold expressionism that defined prairie architecture after Expo '67, associated also with Douglas Cardinal (St. Mary's Church, Red Deer) and Jack Long (Calgary Planetarium). Set on a curving brick base that wraps the programmatic elements of the Roman Catholic mass, a double-helix of glulam wood beams rise and interlace to form the roof structure. Fir decking is set across each wooden beam, and the roof is wrapped in cedar shakes, creating an undulating exterior landscape in sharp contrast to Winnipeg's flatness. Lessons learned from Gaboury inform Helliwell's breakthrough Spiral House on Hornby Island and Fishbones House on Galiano Island. His design education now buttressed by time in an office, Helliwell graduated from the University of Manitoba in 1969.

Helliwell, true to the spirit of his generation, sought his west coast baptism with a visit to San Francisco's Haight-Ashbury neighbourhood in 1968. A visit to a Vancouver aunt on the way led to an immediate connection to the office of Arthur Erickson. He never made it to San Francisco but he did spend four years working with Erickson Massey. Canada's most acclaimed and influential architect of the 20th century, Erickson's practice featured large university and museum buildings in one portion of the practice, while another produced houses that are quiet exemplars of site-sensitive west coast modernism. Working under partner Geoff Massey, Helliwell's first completed house was the Rothstein House in the ski resort of Whistler. With its angular roofs, 'saddle-bag' cantilevered rooms, and board-covered elevations, it is a design clearly inspired by Sea Ranch's condos and other housing projects by Charles Moore of Moore Lyndon Turner

Below: Eglise du Précieux–Sang by architect Etienne Gaboury 1967
Middle: Rothstein House, Whistler designed by Bo Helliwell at Erickson Massey 1970
Bottom: Smith House II, West Vancouver by Erickson Massey 1964

Whittaker in San Francisco. During this period at Erickson Massey, he became friends with Nick Milkovich, who has provided technical and inspirational support for more than 40 years.

Two seemingly contradictory tendencies dominate the post-Erickson portion of Helliwell's career: academic studies during 1972–74 at one of the world's most advanced and intellectual architecture schools – London's Architectural Association – followed by a move in 1975 to the counter-culture haven of Hornby Island, where he started work as a builder and began raising a family. A daughter, Rowan, was born in 1976 and son Zeke in 1981. At the Architectural Association, Helliwell appreciated the perch in Bedford Square, where a changing world and architectural culture in transformation was evident. Helliwell participated in design studios with Bernard Tschumi and Mike Gold, dialogues with Peter Wilson and John Jenner, and started his long association with Australian Brit Andresen, admiring her interest in the art of building, rare at the time. At the Architectural Association then were the various design tendencies associated with phenomenology, the Street Farmers movement (urban agriculture anarchists) and the early beginnings of Post Modernism and Deconstructivism in architecture. Along the way Helliwell got to know many key figures in contemporary architectural culture, but in so doing never lost his interest and commitment to small-scale building.

After the Architectural Association, he travelled overland from London to Thailand with his partner and father, a profound experience on many levels, then on to Vancouver, settling on Hornby Island. *Architectural Design* magazine was closely linked to the Architectural Association school, and in its July 1978 issue Helliwell co-edited an issue on the theme of "Handbuilt Hornby". There are few better exemplars of Helliwell's boundary-breaking thinking than this issue of the magazine, with its praise of community, tales of self-building, deftly wonderful drawings, and the narratives embedded in houses like children under a quilt. The publication promoted the work of Blue Sky Design, which Helliwell had founded with Michael McNamara in 1975 on Hornby Island, and led to their being invited to present at the Berlin International Building Exhibition (IBA) of 1984. Newly partnered with Kim Smith, Helliwell returned to living in Vancouver in 1989, but the couple has always maintained a residence on Hornby. Nearly all their initiatives after this point are collaborations.

KIM SMITH

BIOGRAPHIES

Left: 'Jungle Room', The Licks
Restaurant by Kim Smith and
Nicola Kozakiewicz 1987

Kim Smith was born in 1953 in Kingston, a university and institutional city midway between Montreal and Toronto that was briefly the nation's capital. Her engineer/developer father was a leader in the postwar suburban development of the city, and she grew up in an A-frame modernist house, a rarity in a city that was largely Victorian in outlook and architecture. Smith's undergraduate studies were in Film and English at Queen's University in Kingston. Sailing on Lake Ontario and travel were also early passions, combined when she built a 40-foot catamaran in her early twenties and sailed it to the Caribbean. The catamaran was constructed in the mid-1970s at a rural cabin where 'back to the land' living skills were mastered, leading to a 50-by-30-foot boat shed, her first completed building.

The lure of the landscape and the sailing and skiing potential of Canada's west coast beckoned even before graduation – Kim finished off some of her undergraduate courses at the University of British Columbia (UBC), and in summers supported herself with the back-breaking manual labour of tree-planting in British Columbia's coastal forests. Her interest in architecture began when she worked on a National Film Board film documenting the construction of a solar house in Vancouver Island, followed by the construction of the 40-foot sailboat. This led to an application to study architecture back to UBC, where the catamaran and its boat shed joined photographs and drawings in her successful portfolio. Experimenting in communal living by purchasing a house with other students, her next completed design work was the radical renovation of its coach house as her own studio-cum-abode.

UBC at that time was deeply influenced by two tendencies originating in Berkeley: the modernist regionalism of Bernard Maybeck and his followers in the Pacific Northwest; and the design detail from precedent, promoted by Professor Christopher Alexander. While close to Berkeley ideals, the school then was somewhat estranged from the vital local scene, with such talented teachers as Arthur Erickson and Bruno Freschi being pushed out of the school when their practices thrived. At the time the school was without female representation in the faculty, and Kim Smith continued summer employment by planting trees rather than doing rote work for a local practice in uncertain economic times. An ongoing interest

in play and fantasy, and a questioning of gender roles led to a superficially controversial but deeply considered thesis: a sex club or 'love hotel' on the Japanese model. A reconciliation of radial and jaggedly triangular plan geometries, the formal language of the thesis anticipates first the Deconstructivism of the later 1980s, and points towards the invigoration she brought to the housing designs of Bo Helliwell when they began their collaborations a few years later.

British Columbia's economy is marked by extreme cycles of boom and bust, dictated by the global price of the commodities it produces, and when Smith graduated in 1984, the local architecture scene was being sustained solely by design work for the class II international exhibition on a transportation theme, EXPO '86. Smith contributed to interior designs for fair pavilions by local firms, but soon resolved to supplement her education so that she could more easily work for herself. In the summer of 1985 Kim Smith joined a design studio at the Pratt Institute in New York City. By autumn she had decided to switch to the Architectural Association School in London. One of the oldest architecture schools in the English-speaking world, the Architectural Association was a hotbed of innovation and debate, with teachers and students including Rem Koolhaas, Leon Krier, Zaha Hadid, Steven Holl and others passing through in the decade between when Helliwell studied there and her own London experience. While in London, Smith worked for the highly regarded practice of Anglo-Canadian Trevor Horne, mainly on domestic projects.

After the year in New York and London, Smith returned to the Canadian west coast, her passion for mountain and sea (and the sailing and skiing that goes with them) undiminished by time away. Smith bought a house on Hornby Island and began renovating it, while at the same time pursuing independent design commissions in the city. One of these was the jungle-themed renovation of a West Vancouver restaurant, collaboration with Nikki Kozakiewicz. Long since renovated away, the design announced many of the themes of her subsequent work: bold colour, a playful spatial sense, and a seductiveness of surface and texture. After this she spent some time working in the office of A.A. Robins, but by 1987 was based wholly on Hornby Island.

KIM AND BO

BIOGRAPHIES

Kim Smith began working with the then Hornby Island-based Blue Sky Design and Bo Helliwell in 1987. They collaborated on design projects as their relationship evolved into being both partners in work and partners in life. Early joint creations while based on Hornby were located there and on adjacent Denman Island and the nearby shores of Vancouver Island. Several years later, they decided to re-locate to the city, a decision based as much on their personal, intellectual and social needs as business opportunities.

By settling into a house-based practice located in West Vancouver, Bo's two children, Rowan and Zeke, were able to join them in West Vancouver for secondary school years. This location maintained close links to the ferry system to Hornby and the other Islands, and easy access to the new resort of Whistler, where this skiing couple owned a vacation condo that Helliwell had worked on while working for Erickson-Massey. Their arrival back was followed by an exhibition of Blue Sky Design's creations at Simon Fraser University sponsored by the Vancouver League for Studies in Architecture and the Environment. This was a fertile time for both Helliwell and Smith, with an expansion of the range of their designs and personal interests. They set up their West Vancouver residence and home office in the notable 1964 Fawkes House designed by leading regionalist-modernist Barry Downs and expanded their zone of design commissions to Whistler and the Southern Gulf Islands.

Both started teaching architecture part-time at the University of British Columbia, as well as working with the Vancouver League, a non-profit group, bringing international lectures, competitions and exhibitions to Vancouver. Through these exchanges, they built on their previous London exposure to leading edge design from around the world. They would frequently host these international architectural guests at their Hornby home, leading naturally to reciprocal invitations to speak and visit in other countries. For example, they built on their London Architectural Association links with Brit Andersen to invite her for several speaking engagements in Vancouver, which led to visits to Queensland, and further links to Lindsay and Karrie Clare, among others. Similar links to Carlos Mijares of Mexico City and Carlos Morales of Bogota led to visits there and repeated teaching engagements at his ISTHMUS private architecture school in Panama. Other international travel was motivated by curiosity, such as tours of Bhutan, India, Japan, Africa, China, South America and Europe.

Both Smith and Helliwell have served and continue to serve local communities by serving as architect members of West Vancouver's design panel (a peer review system charged to improve the quality of design). Helliwell served on the provincial council of the Architectural Institute of British Columbia from 1996 to 2001, and in 2012 was made a Fellow of the Royal Architectural Institute of Canada. Travel and guest lecturing have brought them to five continents, all the while using their Hornby and Whistler homes to host designers and writers from many countries.

Bit by bit, their work was published in such magazines as London's *Architecture Review*, Milan's *Casabella*, Vancouver's *Western Living*, and Toronto's *Canadian Architect*. Working with Vancouver architecture critic Trevor Boddy as editor, in 1998 they published the first monograph on their design work, produced by Images Publishing of Australia. The book and increased coverage in the North American design and lifestyle press led to an increase in house commissions, especially of larger size and greater budget. In 1998, they bought a second Barry Downs-designed house, adding a studio wing on to it to serve as the permanent base of Blue Sky Architecture, the new company being inaugurated in 1992. Their office expanded over this time and in 2000 they designed and built their own working studio, sited around an existing garden next to their home. By intention, staff has been limited to between two and five employees, with the integration and work possible at that scale and from that singular place.

After 2000, multi-family housing and small public buildings became part of their practice, but Blue Sky Architecture never sought the collaborations with large firms necessary for bigger projects, preferring to limit commissions to a number and scale where a consistency of quality was possible. Work also expanded with new project types: multi-family projects, commercial projects, public projects and projects in the USA and further afield in Canada – in Winnipeg and Ontario. This increased scope of building types and locales inspired a different look to the architecture, though the principles they had developed over time informed these projects in concept and reality. Despite the buffeting of economic upswings and downswings they have continued with a steady evolution of work to a mature understanding of architecture.

BLUE SKY
ARCHITECTURE
1990–2012

STAFF ARCHITECTS AND DESIGNERS

Bettina Balcaen

Andrew Best

Chelsea Bourke

Sarah Brar

Dominique Cameron

Elena Chernyshov

Mark Erickson

David Garrioch

Raphael Gomez

Bo Helliwell

Steve Hinton

Philip Van Horne

Nicola Kozakiewicz

Matt Macleod

Catherine MacQuarrie

Rob McGill

Lindsay Nette

Richard Peck

Simon Pirquet

Tobias Pond

Bruce Ramsay

Volker Ritter

Kim Smith

Amy Stein

Elise Young

CONSULTANTS AND BUILDERS

3D Joinery – Dan Anderson

AFC Construction – Alan Fletcher

Alta Lake Lumber – Glen Lynskey

Blue Sky Design – Michael McNamara and Tim Wyndham

Boda Construction – Brian Boyd

Chiu Hippmann Engineering – Carlos Chiu, Tim Hippmann

G Speed Construction – Gord Speed

Merlin Construction – Paul Summerlin

Mike Forester Construction – Mike Forester

Perez Engineering – Willie Perez

R Parsons Construction – Rob Parsons

Sound Building & Design – Peter Stade

Toredo Woodworks – John Grunewald

Zeke Helliwell Designs – Zeke Helliwell

We have limited this list to those who have worked for the firm for a significant period of time. To those listed above and the many people whose names do not appear here,

Thank you

SELECTED BIBLIOGRAPHY

HELLIWELL + SMITH • BLUE SKY ARCHITECTURE PUBLICATIONS

Browne, Beth, *Masterpiece: Iconic Houses by Great Contemporary Architects*, Images Publishing Group, Mulgrave, Victoria, Australia, 2012, pp. 140–145.

Coast Modern, HD, directed by Gavin Froome and Mike Bernard, Twofold Films, Vancouver, 2012.

Cleary, Mark, *200 Houses*, Images Publishing Group, Mulgrave, Victoria, Australia, 2010, pp. 228–229 and 500–503.

Hall, Andrew, "Elma Bay Residence", *21st Century Beach Houses*. Images Publishing Group, Mulgrave, Victoria, Australia, 2010, pp. 68–71.

Helliwell, Bo & Smith, Kim, "House for Booklovers", *Wood Design & Building*. Spring 2010, pp. 10–14.

Kalman, Harold & Ward, Robin, "Harbour House", *Exploring Vancouver*, Douglas & McIntrye, Vancouver, Canada, 2010, pp. 242, 266–76.

Browne, Beth, *100 Country Houses*, Images Publishing Group, Mulgrave, Victoria, Australia, 2009, pp. 240–241 and 264–267.

Costa, Sergi & Eguaras, Mariana E., "An international survey of Architectural Ideas", *1000 Ideas by 100 Architects*, Rockport Publishers, Beverly, MA, USA, 2009, pp. 178–181.

Costa, Sergi, "Beach Homes on South Chesterman", *Private Residential Complexes*, Loft Publications, Barcelona, Spain, 2008, pp. 182–189.

Costa, Sergi, "Casas en South Chesterman", *Complejos Residenciales Privados*, Instituto Monsa de Ediciones, Barcelona, Spain, 2007, pp. 182–189.

Gordon, Alastair, "Handbuilt Hornby Island", *Spaced Out: Radical Environments of the Psychedelic Sixties*, Rizzoli, New York, USA, 2008, pp. 270–275.

Moreno, Esther & Vranckx, Bridget, "South Chesterman Beach Homes", *200 Outstanding House Ideas*. Loft Publications, Barcelona, 2008, pp. 694–703.

Symons, Christina, *1000 x Architecture of the Americas*. Verlagshaus Braun, Berlin, 2008, pp. 12–16 and 64.

Crosbie, Michael J., *Architecture for Architects*, Images Publishing Group, Mulgrave, Victoria, Australia, 2007, pp. 144–147.

Porteous, Colin, with MacGregor, Kerr, "Solar Houses & Sustainable Architecture", *Solar Architecture in Cool Climates*, Earthscan, London, 2005.

Smith, Will, "The Murphy House", *The New Modern House: Case Studies of 40 New Houses*, Princeton Architectural Press, New York, USA, 2005, pp. 100–103.

The Poetics of West Coast Modernism in West Vancouver (Catalogue and exhibition), the Ferry Building Gallery, Silk Purse Gallery and West Vancouver Library Galley, West Vancouver, 2005.

Braghieri, Nicola, *Case in Legno* (an international survey of Wooden Houses), Fedrico Motta Editore, Milan, 2004, pp. 172–195.

Living Spaces, (Catalogue of a national exhibition of 21 contemporary Canadian homes), Cambridge Galleries, Cambridge, Ontario, 2004.

Noal, Sarah, "Mike's House", *Cool Architecture*, Images Publishing Group, Mulgrave, Victoria, Australia, 2003, pp. 86–91.

Residential Spaces of the World, Volume 5, Images Publishing Group, Mulgrave, Victoria, Australia, 2003.

Davis, Jodie & Strong, Diane, "Greenwood House", *100 of the World's Best Houses*, Images Publishing Group, Mulgrave, Victoria, Australia, 2002, pp. 132–133.

Mostaedi, Arian, "Greenwood House" and "Fishbones House", *New Coastal Houses*, Instituto Monsa de Ediciones, Barcelona, Spain, 2001.

Home Front in the Garden (BBC television production featuring Blue Sky Architecture and Arthur Erickson), 2001.

Adamcyzk, Georges, *Maisons-lieux/Houses-Places* (Catalogue of national exhibition of contemporary Canadian architecture), La Biennale de Montreal, 2000.

Nicholls, Jim, "Framed Views", *Arcade*, vol. 18, no. 3, Spring 2000, pp. 30–31.

Rowlands, Penelope, *Weekend Houses*, Chronicle Books, San Francisco, 2000.

Architects of the New Millennium, Images Publishing Group, Mulgrave, Victoria, Australia, 2000, pp. 104–105.

"Blue Sky Architecture: Casa Fishbones", *Casabella 680*, Anno LXIV July–August, 2000, p. 28.

Residential Spaces of the World, Volume 4, Images Publishing Group, Mulgrave, Victoria, Australia, 2000, pp 46–47, 56–57, 94–95, 99, 165, 170, 218.

Boddy, Trevor, *Picturesque, Tectonic, Romantic: Helliwell+Smith, Blue Sky Architecture*, Images Publishing Group, Mulgrave, Victoria, Australia, 1999.

Davey, Peter, "Fishbones House", *Architectural Review*, January 1997.

Blomeyer, Gerald, "Savage Dreams", *Architectural Review*, February 1988, pp. 27–33.

"A House for Today", *Architectural Design*, vol. 56, November 1986, p. 25.

Blomeyer, Gerald & Tietze, Barbara, *Die Andere Bauarbeit* (Alternative Building), Deutsche Verlags-Anstalt, Berlin, Germany, 1984, pp. 54–59.

Chaitkin, Wiliam & Jencks, Charles, "Alternatives", *Architecture Today*, 1982, pp. 225–259.

Helliwell, Bo & McNamara, Michael, "Handbuilt Hornby", *Architectural Design*, vol. 48, no. 7, 1978, pp. 443–491.

ACKNOWLEDGEMENTS

Bo Helliwell and Kim Smith would like to express their thanks for their rich and varied life in architecture and the opportunities and connections that architecture has created for them, with wonderful people, beautiful places, opportunities to keep learning and exploring and for challenging and fun projects and problems. A gift of great friendships has come through living with architecture, with co-workers, colleagues, builders, crafts people, clients, family and this beautiful earth.

We would particularly like to thank the people who have helped us put this book together: Trevor Boddy for his insight, intelligence and humour, Ted Cullinan for his generous visit from another planet, Elena Chernyshov for her management, graphic skills and tenacity, Images Publishing for the opportunity to produce another book, and Barry Downs for his generosity and continued inspiration. We extend a special thanks to all of our co-workers, builders and the clients listed here and the many not listed, for their inspiration, sense of adventure and trust.

CLIENTS

Don and Vivian Chan

Allan and Benedicte Cockell

Bruce Fairbairne

Julie Glover

Nikki and Pip Graham

Barry and Sophie Greenwood

Robin and Janet Halliwell

Barbara and Jim Harvey

John and Caroline Hopley

Chris Lefevre

Charles Loewen

Cheryl Loewen

Marilyn and Ian MacBeath

Margo McKay

Paul and Holly McNally

Jan and Peter Murphy

Paula Palyga and David Demers

Derek Riley

Jim and Judy Saks

Chris and Carol Schneider

Lance Sparling

Jennifer Talbot and Michael Tory

The Ucluelet Aquarium Society

PHOTOGRAPHY CREDITS

Blue Sky Archives 8, 9, 10 (top left, top middle), 12, 13, 14, 15 (left), 18, 25, 27, 29 (top), 31 (top left), 38, 39 (top, bottom), 40, 42, 46, 47 (top), 48, 49, 52 (middle), 57 (left), 58 (bottom right), 61, 62, 63, 65 (bottom right), 66, 67 (top left), 69 (bottom right), 71 (bottom), 76 (middle right, lower middle right), 77, 84, 86, 87 (top), 89, 91 (bottom right), 95 (bottom), 96, 97, 98, 100, 101 (top), 102, 103, 108 (top left), 117, 118 (right), 121 (top left, top right), 126 (top left, bottom left), 127, 128 (top), 131 (top, bottom right), 135, 139, 140, 143 (bottom), 144, 145

Edward Cullinan Architects 7

David Delnea 138, 141 (bottom)

Barry Downs 11

Ron Faleide 37, 41, 43

Brice Ferré 23

Alan Fletcher 88 (bottom left)

John Fulker 88 (bottom right), 91 (top, bottom left), 93, 110, 111, 112, 113 (right), 115 (middle, bottom), 122, 143 (middle)

Gaboury archives 143 (top)

Vince Klassen 104, 105, 106, 108 (top middle, top right, bottom), 109

Gerry Kopelow 128 (bottom), 129, 130, 131 (bottom left), 132

Michael McNamara 123 (top)

Patrizia Menton 113 (left)

Heath Moffatt 118 (left), 119, 120, 121 (bottom)

Christopher Pouget 44, 45, 47 (bottom), 50, 52 (top, bottom), 53

Peter Powles 15 (right), 17, 19, 64, 65, 75, 76 (top, bottom right), 78, 79, 87 (bottom), 88 (top), 90, 101 (bottom left), 115 (top), 123 (bottom left), 124, 125, 126 (right), 136, 137

Gillean Proctor 29 (bottom), 31 (top right, bottom), 32, 33, 34, 55, 56, 57 (right), 58 (top, bottom left), 59, 67 (top right, bottom), 69 (top, bottom left), 70, 71 (top), 72, 73, 80, 81, 82, 85, 95 (top left, top right), 101 (bottom right)

Oscar Sieg 123 (bottom right)

Christina Symons 141 (top)

Martin Tessler 20, 21